FAMILY
FORAGING

Author's note on safety

Foraging is not without its risks, and as a responsible adult it is up to you to manage those risks for yourself and your family. The thirty plants and mushrooms listed here have been carefully chosen and represent some of the most straightforward wild foods you can find. They are a great introduction to foraging for even the youngest wild food enthusiast. You know your children better than I do, so you will know the extent of their abilities and the level of supervision they need. Some will grab a book like this and be utterly sensible, others less so. It pays to never under- or overestimate a child's ability, but to understand the risks and manage them well. Please read "How to forage safely" (page 12) thoroughly.

Disclaimer

Although every reasonable effort has been made to ensure all the information in this book is correct as of the date of its publication, the author and publisher do not assume responsibility for and hereby exclude to the fullest extent possible by law, any and all liability for any loss, damage, injury, illness, or loss of life caused by negligence (including incorrect information in this book) or mistakes in the interpretation of the information in this book. Reliance on the information in this book is at the sole risk of the reader. In short, if you pick something, it is your responsibility!

Roost Books
An imprint of Shambhala Publications, Inc.
4720 Walnut Street
Boulder, Colorado 80301
roostbooks.com

First published in 2019
by White Lion Publishing,
an imprint of The Quarto Group.
The Old Brewery, 6 Blundell Street
London, N7 9BH,
United Kingdom
T (0)20 7700 6700
www.QuartoKnows.com

Text © 2019 David Hamilton
Photography © 2019 Jason Ingram,
except where stated otherwise.
Illustrations © 2019 Sara Mulvanny

David Hamilton has asserted his moral right to be identified as the Author
of this Work in accordance with the Copyright Designs and Patents Act 1988.

9 8 7 6 5 4 3 2 1

First U.S. Edition

Printed in China

Every effort has been made to trace the copyright holders of material quoted in this book. If application is made in writing to the publisher, any omissions will be included in future editions.

Design by Sarah Pyke

Roost Books is distributed worldwide by Penguin Random House, Inc., and its subsidiaries.

Library of Congress Cataloging-in-Publication Data
Names: Hamilton, Dave, 1974- author.
Title: Family foraging: a fun guide to gathering and eating wild plants / David Hamilton.
Description: First U.S. edition. | Boulder: Shambhala, 2019. | Includes index.
Identifiers: LCCN 2018037731 | ISBN 9781611806847 (paperback: alk. paper)
Subjects: LCSH: Wild plants, Edible. | Cooking (Wild foods)
Classification: LCC QK98.5.A1 H365 2019 | DDC 581.6/32—dc23
LC record available at https://lccn.loc.gov/2018037731

MIX
Paper from
responsible sources
FSC® C101537
www.fsc.org

FAMILY
FORAGING

A fun guide to gathering and eating wild plants

DAVID HAMILTON

PHOTOGRAPHY BY JASON INGRAM

ROOST BOOKS
BOULDER
2019

CONTENTS

6 Foraging Basics
8 Introduction
10 Why Forage?
12 How to Forage Safely
13 What to Wear and What to Bring
14 Where to Forage
22 What you Need in the Kitchen
23 Conservation

24 Spring
26 Nettle
30 Dandelion
34 Wild Ramps
38 Goosefoot
42 Chickweed
44 Spearmint
48 Garlic Mustard
52 Plantain

54 Summer
56 Wild Cherry
60 Elder
64 Wild Blueberry
68 Virginia Glasswort
70 Sheep's Sorrel
74 Giant Puffball
78 Wild Radish
80 Virginian Strawberry
84 Wild Plum
88 Blackberry

92 Fall
94 Apple
98 Rose
102 Hawthorn
106 Black Raspberry
110 Beech
112 Cep
116 Hazelnut
120 Sweet Chestnut
124 Staghorn Sumac

128 Winter
130 Wood Sorrel
132 Sea Beet
136 Birch

140 Index
142 About the Author
142 Thanks To
143 Picture Credits

FORAGING
BASICS

Foraging can be a great way to connect
as a family and get back in touch with
the natural world. Getting started is simple.
Discover what makes foraging so fun as
you learn where to go, what to bring,
and how to do it safely.

INTRODUCTION

Like many others, my experience of wild foods began when I was very young. I grew up quite far from the "wild," in a large town. I craved the outdoors, and along with my brother and sister we would find our own wild places among our otherwise urban surroundings; we picked elderberries for jams and nettles for soup from the bottom of our garden, we ate beech nuts from the large beech tree in the corner of our school playground, and on family days out we all picked blackberries together. The blackberries were picked with pies and jams in mind, but they seldom made it home, as we munched away at them, staining our fingers and tops with the delicious juice.

The older I got, the more fascinated I became with plants, and my knowledge grew. With no internet and few books on the subject it was a difficult thing to study, and this book represents what I would have liked to have read back then. Within these pages you will find thirty of the most straightforward plants, fruits, nuts, and mushrooms to forage in the Northern Hemisphere. Hopefully there will be some you already know, but no doubt some will be new to you. Included with the entries are delicious recipes to make at home and interesting facts to tell your friends.

At this point I feel I should give you, the reader, a warning. You may think that I should warn you that you need to be 100% sure of what you are picking. It is a good one to start with, as putting any old plant or mushroom in your mouth might not be your best idea ever (in fact, it could be your last); some plants and mushrooms can make you very sick indeed, and some may even kill you. However, that's not the biggest warning that should go with this book. No, the biggest is this . . .

. . . WARNING: FORAGING IS FOR LIFE!

Once you get the foraging bug, there is no turning back. As soon as summer ends you will be asking yourself: where can I find chestnuts to roast, hazelnuts to crack, or the best wild apple trees? During the cold winter days, you'll be searching the coast for overwintering sea beet leaves. Spring will be met with a newfound anticipation for the first shoots of ramps/wild garlic or fresh, early nettles waking up from their winter slumber. Then, as summer finally comes around again, you will want to spend as much time as you can outside, hunting for the sweet taste of summer berries. There is little to compare with the flavor of the first succulent blackberry or the first cherry plum hanging over onto the street from an overgrown spooky garden.

A word for parents and caregivers

From Darwin to David Attenborough, many naturalists built their careers on a fascination with nature which began in early childhood. However, in this digital age our children can all too easily become isolated from meaningful contact with both the natural world and the adults around them. Foraging for wild food can help alleviate this; a day gathering blackberries can be a great way to reconnect as a family and with the great outdoors.

Throughout the book there are facts about some of the plants to help widen a child's botanical knowledge. I can't claim your child will be the next Charles Darwin, but I can say that it might encourage them to do something other than watch TV or play on a tablet all day!

WHY FORAGE?

You may ask, "Why do I need to forage at all? Surely everything I eat can be bought in the supermarket?"

Well, yes, it can, but head to any supermarket, anywhere in the world, and you pretty much know you'll find the same basic things. Where's the fun in that? Besides, who has ever had an adventure in a supermarket? Can you recall a book called *Charlie the Champion of the Cheese Counter* or *Harry Potter and the Chamber of Frozen Sausages*?!

For the adventure

When you set foot outside your front door looking for wild foods, an adventure begins. You never really know what you are going to find, how much of it you are going to bring home, or what is going to happen that day. Perhaps you will find an apple tree so laden with fruit that you can fill your belly and your bag to the bursting point! Or maybe Dad will sting himself on a patch of nettles or tumble into a bramble patch trying to get the juiciest blackberry . . .

The whole family can join in

Both my children could identify blackberries before they could talk (always under supervision). There is no real lower or upper age limit, so foraging is something you can do with friends and relatives from 0–90 and beyond.

No more boring days out

Foraging not only brings a little adventure into your life, it also brings a purpose to what could otherwise

BY YOUR OWN HAND

Food you have found yourself is so much more appealing. I know one six-year-old who won't eat anything green served to him, but put him in a field of sorrel and he will happily munch all day!

have been quite a boring day out. It means you aren't just walking to an old church that Mum wants to visit; you are a hunter-gatherer for the day, just like your prehistoric ancestors!

Freshness

Although they look fresh, the apples you buy in a supermarket could be anywhere from six months to a year old. Even salad bags could be at least a week, or even up to a month old before you buy them. The longer you leave any natural food product, the more the vitamins and minerals it contains start to break down. Wild food is fresh, *really fresh*—sometimes only seconds or minutes old—meaning it is packed full of goodness.

Cost

One of the best things about wild food is that it is completely and utterly free. Some of the entries in this book, such as the porcini or *boletus* mushroom (also known as cep or penny bun), are very expensive indeed if bought. Some people make money picking wild mushrooms and wild plants and selling them to restaurants or markets; these places charge a lot of money for the privilege of eating food you can pick for absolutely nothing.

HOW TO FORAGE SAFELY

Be 100% certain: This first point is very important. **Never, ever, ever, ever eat a plant or mushroom unless you are 100% sure of what it is.**

Don't dive in: Try not to dive into this book looking for the strangest things to pick first. Start by simply looking at the entries for familiar fruits such as apples, plums, cherries, and blackberries. Once you have built up your confidence with the familiar foods, then start looking for those that are less familiar to you.

Read the descriptions thoroughly: Although the plant identification photographs in this book go some way to showing you what a wild food looks like, it is also important to read the descriptions. You will find tips on identifying the plant or mushroom along with details of any poisonous lookalikes.

Local guides: Ask members of your family or friends with a good knowledge of wild food to come with you on your first forays. Also, look for guided wild food walks in your area.

Get a local guide book: There is a thriving market for wild food, wildflower and mushroom guides, both on the internet and in thrift stores. Pick up some for your region; they will help as your interest in foraging and wild plants grows.

Use the internet: Each entry has a common and a scientific name: for example, chickweed is *Stellaria media*, and nettle is *Urtica dioica*. Type these names into a search engine and you will see many pictures of the plant, fruit, nut, or mushroom you are looking for.

Allergic reactions: You never quite know how you might react to a completely new food. To check you are not allergic, put a tiny bit in your mouth, bite down on it, then spit it out. Wait an hour then try a little more. If you are fine, eat and swallow a larger piece, say teaspoon-sized, then repeat this the following day. If you have no reaction then the food is safe for you. There is no need to do this for foods you have had before, such as apples or plums.

Take what you need: Only ever pick what you need; humans aren't the only creatures who eat wild foods so be sure to leave enough for the birds, caterpillars, and mice!

Wash your food: Wash your food before you eat it. This will get rid of any bugs, both microscopic ones which can make you sick, and large ones which might ruin the taste of what you are eating. If you pick where dogs have been walked, wash and cook whatever you pick.

Pollution: Don't pick by the side of the road or near factories, areas which can be quite polluted. Also, don't pick in graveyards as the lead from the coffins can get into the wild plants, and especially mushrooms.

WHAT TO WEAR AND WHAT TO BRING

Boots: You'll need a good pair of walking boots if you are hiking to find your food. By the sea or near rivers, waterproof boots are essential.

Raincoat: Ideal for staying dry and warm.

Sun hat and sunglasses: To protect from the sun—and of course to look good!

Protective gloves: A good pair of gardening gloves protect hands from nettle stings and thorns.

Long pants: Especially useful where legs may get stung or scratched.

Books and phone apps: Local field guides and phone apps help to identify plants while you get to know them.

Scissors: Great for cutting nettles and greens.

Bags and containers: Always bring along a good selection of plastic and paper bags, old takeout cartons, and reusable plastic boxes to carry home your foraged goodies.

Berry picker: A useful tool for bilberries and fruit with small branches. It has bended comblike teeth at the front for scooping, and can be found online and in specialist outdoor stores.

First-aid kit: Cuts and bruises are part of the experience, and it always helps to be prepared.

Bottle of water: Foraging can be thirsty work.

Snacks for a picnic or foods to go with foraged food: A simple lunch such as bread and cheese can be supplemented with foraged salad and fruit.

Sunscreen: Essential for protection on a sunny day.

WHERE TO FORAGE

THE COAST

Plants by the coast have to be a lot tougher than those inland. Look at the leaves of coastal plants; they are often thick and waxy to enable them to deal with the strong winds and salty air. Sea beet, for example, has much thicker leaves than its beet relative. Some trees have wider gaps between their branches to allow the coastal gusts to blow through them, while palm trees can bend in high winds without breaking. Common trees, such as hawthorn, are shaped by high winds, making them look as if they have been caught in a giant hairdryer. As an added protection from coastal gusts, some plants can grow close to or along the ground in what's known as a "prostrate" form. There is a type of goosefoot that does just this, crawling flat across the sand, and its leaves have a surprisingly salty taste.

How to forage there

Look in the dunes, along headlands, and in the banks surrounding the beaches away from the shoreline. Virginia glasswort only grows in tidal marsh estuaries, so be sure to check tide times and only walk in the mud if it is safe to do so. Always wash and cook any low-lying coastal plants if dogs are walked in the area. If you hear of sewage contaminating your local beach, it would be unwise to forage there (though thankfully this is rare). Never reach further than is safe to forage; fences are there for a reason and it is never worth tumbling off a cliff for the sake of supper!

What to find there

Goosefoot, Plantain, Virginia glasswort, Wild radish, Sea beet, Rose, Giant puffball (on headlands), Hawthorn, Beach plums.

WOODLANDS AND FORESTS

A woodland can provide a welcome break from the sun on a hot summer's day, and a magical place to spend time with the family. Food plants inhabit every niche, from clover-like wood sorrel on the forest floor, to brambles clambering their way into trees, and chestnuts growing high in the canopy. Even the smallest copse of trees can be host to countless edibles, with wild raspberries taking advantage of any gaps in the canopy, mushrooms feeding on the roots of the trees, and a great mix of plants on the outward fringes. During the spring, the first bright green leaves of birch, hawthorn, lime, and beech are all edible. If the branches are low enough, or you have some shoulders to sit on top of, you can munch the leaves straight from the tree like a giraffe (but watch out for thorns).

How to forage there
Begin searching for wild food plants along the outward edges of the woodland; blackberries, raspberries, and woodland strawberries prefer these lighter areas rather than the dark interior. Mushrooms are also often found on the outer fringes, or on the edge of clearings, rather than deep within the woods. Always wear good boots and long pants, as woods can be muddy and there are often low-growing plants which can scratch or sting (or even trip you up). Look down for beech nuts, chestnuts, and hazelnuts during the fall; you may be able to shake the tree for more.

What to find there
Nettle (woodland edges), Ramps/Wild garlic, Elder, Woodland strawberry, Blackberry, Raspberry, Beech, Ceps, Birch, Hazelnut, Hawthorn, Mint (near water), Wild plum, Chestnut, Garlic mustard.

PARKS, GARDENS, AND PUBLIC SPACES

The local park is a great place to start a foraging adventure. During the spring and summer, search the wild corners for edible weeds and blackberries. Once you have adopted a forager's eye, you will find food plants simply everywhere. You can often find wild roses and sumac trees in public areas such as supermarket parking lots or municipal planting areas. I never visit a grand house or stately home without looking for fallen chestnuts, windfall apples, or woodland strawberries. In fact, if I am not careful I can spend a day looking at my feet! In some states and countries foraging in public parks is prohibited, so always check the local law.

How to forage there

Not all parks and gardens are the same, nor do they have the same rules. It should go without saying that it would not be wise to pick apples, plums, or pears from the orchard of a stately home (although windfalls should be fine), but I doubt if anyone would mind if you picked up their chickweed. You should never forage in a private garden without permission, although legally there is no harm in picking an apple from a branch hanging over into a public street. Avoid any plants that are yellow, heavily wilting, or appear to be dying, as it is likely these have been sprayed with weed killer.

What to find there

Nettle, Dandelion, Chickweed, Goosefoot, Mint, Plantain, Cherry, Elder, Blueberry, Sorrel, Giant puffball, Woodland strawberry, Plum, Blackberry, Apple, Rose, Hawthorn, Hazel, Raspberry, Hazelnut, Garlic mustard.

MOORS, PLAINS, AND HEATHS

If your family is willing to have a little adventure, there is nowhere quite like great wide open spaces for a week away. In many countries these are the only areas where wild camping is permitted. With little or no light pollution, spending a night under the stars tucking into sausages and blanched wild greens picked earlier that evening can be a highlight of a well-spent summer vacation. Although their soils lack enough goodness to sustain many larger plants, grassy plains, heaths, and windswept moors are oddly exciting places to hunt for wild foods. To the untrained eye these seem like a totally barren landscape, yet finding a large swathe of blueberry bushes can be a really exhilarating experience.

How to forage there

Many weeds retreat to the edges of walls and the boundaries of fields for protection, so these are always good places to start looking. Even if camping is allowed, never start a fire on land with peaty soil; instead, place a burner or cooking stove on top of a flat rock to prepare your food. Trees can grow sparsely in these areas, and the fruit, especially wild apples, can be quite small. It is important to remember wildlife no matter where you are, however it is especially vital here that you only take what you need, leaving enough for the local animals.

What to find there

Sorrel, Bilberry, Blueberry, Blackberry, Nettle, Dandelion, Plantain, Chickweed, trees along edges or in patches such as Hawthorn, Elder, Apple.

EDGELAND

Edgeland describes places that are neither rural (countryside and wilderness) or urban (towns and cities), but somewhere in between the two. They may be places that were once managed but have been left to go wild. Often called "wastelands," these could be the banks of canals, the sides of roads, small patches of trees, old quarries, or long-abandoned railroads. The word can also describe places with pockets of land which are managed by people, but also have large wild areas such as urban farms, community gardens, or scraps of land running along the backs of houses. These are often very near residential areas and, apart from our own backyards, are often the easiest wild places to get to.

How to forage there
Edgelands are some of the most abundant of all foraging areas, as they can include both native plants and those which have escaped from gardens, such as sumac trees, self-seeded apples, plums, cherries, and raspberry runners. It is important to take care in these areas as they can be places where thoughtless people have dumped their trash, and there may be unforeseen hazards hidden by the undergrowth.

What to find there
Nettle, Blackberry, Plantain, Elder, Goosefoot, Chickweed, Hawthorn, Cherry, Woodland Strawberry, Wild plum, Ramps/Wild garlic, Sumac, Apple, Rose, Raspberry, Beech, Hazelnut, Sweet chestnut, Giant puffball (roadside), Garlic mustard.

FARMLAND, MEADOWS, AND HEDGEROWS

A hedgerow describes the line of shrubs surrounding a farmland, lanes, and roads. They are key areas for wildlife; home to nesting birds, an important refuge for small mammals, and an important site for the country forager. Time-lapse films of bustling hedgerows show these are not peaceful places but a botanical Serengeti, a survival of the fittest as different plants compete for space, food, and light. On organic farms where the weeds grow a little more freely, edible plants grow side by side with the farmer's crops. Goosefoot is a prime example of a farmland weed, but nettle, dandelion, plantain, and chickweed can all be found growing among the crops or along the field boundaries.

How to forage there
Look for plantain next to gates where cows have compacted the ground. Find chickweed, puffballs, and sorrel in open fields, and apple, hawthorn, elder, rose, and hazel in the hedgerows. It is important to stick to public footpaths and legal rights of way when foraging on farmland. If in doubt, ask the land owner for permission. Plants take up exhaust fumes, so avoid picking by busy roads. Also, avoid picking when the farmer is spraying or spreading manure.

What to find there
Nettle, Dandelion, Goosefoot, Hawthorn, Sorrel, Plantain, Blackberry, Elder, Chickweed, Cherry, Goosefoot, Wild plum, Ramps/Wild garlic, Apple, Rose, Beech, Hazel, Giant puffball, Garlic mustard.

WHAT YOU NEED IN THE KITCHEN

Sieve, muslin cloth, coffee filters: Wild foods can be accompanied by all sorts of things you will want to filter out, such as seeds, tiny hairs, or even bugs. Each recipe will suggest which of these is best to use.

Saucepan: Essential for sauces, soups, and purées.

Measuring jug: Look for a jug which measures both fluid ounces (fl oz) and milliliters (ml); all recipes use both of these measurements.

Measuring spoons/cups: A set of measuring spoons/cups comes in very handy for recipes; they accurately measure teaspoons, half teaspoons, tablespoons, and cups. If you don't have any, remember the following basic guide:
3 teaspoons = 1 tablespoon;
13 tablespoons = 1 cup.

Scales: You'll need to weigh some of the ingredients for the recipes; measurements are given in both ounces and grams.

Cupcake liners: Not essential, but they do make it easier to remove muffins from the tin.

Baking tray: Both a flat baking tray for pastries, and a cupped one for muffins.

Colander: It is important to wash any bugs or nasties off your foraged ingredients before preparing them.

CONSERVATION

Imagine if you couldn't just dash to the nearest supermarket if you ran out of food. What if every morning your very survival depended on the nuts, berries, mushrooms, and leaves you found in the wild? Or what if you went looking for enough hazelnuts to keep your family alive over winter but the trees had been stripped bare?

This is the struggle that animals, birds, and insects have every day. It is important to consider all forms of wildlife, as they rely on what they can find in the wild. To them it is not "wild food," it is just "food."

So how do we do this and still have enough food for ourselves?

Take only what you need

Well, firstly, only ever pick either what you need, or what you think you will get around to using. A bag full of sweet chestnuts might seem like a great idea, but once you've scored a cross into your fiftieth one they can get a little tedious!

Share and share alike

Often it is easy to share with wildlife without even thinking. For example, it is likely you will only pick elderberries, cherries, and apples from the lower branches, leaving the tops of the trees to the birds. Or you might pick only the tops of nettles or just take a few leaves from a sea beet or wild garlic plant, leaving the rest to grow. Try not to uproot a plant or damage the branches of a tree when you pick from it.

Choose your plant

A good rule of thumb is, if something is abundant (e.g. common weeds like nettle, dandelion, or plantain) then it is unlikely we will decimate the population of them by picking enough for a soup or salad. If something is scarce (e.g. cep/penny bun mushrooms or Virginia glasswort), we should show a little restraint and leave enough for the local wildlife.

SPRING

Emerging fresh green leaves are at their most delicious and nutritious during the spring. Look for the first shoots of nettle and goosefoot along with distinctive dandelion leaves.

NETTLE *URTICA DIOICA*

The nettle is a common herb with stinging hairs and toothed leaves. It grows in patches, with a number of plants clumped together, can reach around 1 ft (30 cm) high, but can grow as tall as 5 ft (1½ m), or even 6½ ft (2 m).

Leaves
The leaves have toothed edges and grow opposite each other on the stem, to a length of ¾–6 in (2–15 cm).

Flowers
Occasionally you will see the "flowers"; these don't look much like flowers, but fuzzy greenish or brownish clusters which droop down from the stem.

Other characteristics
Stems are upright, and square or flat-sided. The stem and the underside of the leaves are covered in tiny stinging hairs.

What to avoid
Plants with round stems or hairless plants lacking a sting. Drooping or discolored plants may have been sprayed. Only pick small plants or the top few leaves (see "A Gritty Taste" on page 29).

Where in the world?
Common in cooler, wetter countries. Found throughout the United States, Canada, and Europe.

Where to find it locally
Nettles like rich, moist soil. They grow on wasteland, on the edges of woods, in parks and gardens, and all over the countryside.

HOW TO EAT IT

The first thing you need to do with nettles is sort out those pesky stinging hairs by either drying out the nettles thoroughly or blanching them in hot water. The hairs don't disappear, but they droop and are no longer capable of piercing the skin, delivering their painful mix of chemicals. Always wear thick gardening gloves when picking or handling nettles. The sting will hurt at first and can itch for hours afterwards.

Dried or fresh nettles can be steeped in boiling water and drunk as a tea. Cooked nettle has a lovely, almost nutty flavor and can be used as a replacement for spinach. It goes well with butter, cream cheese, nutmeg, olive oil, or lemon juice. It also makes a rather nice soup when mixed with leek and potato.

GARLICKY NETTLE PESTO

Ingredients

- a colander full of nettles (use tongs or gardening gloves to handle the nettles)
- $^{2}/_{3}$ cup (100 g / 3½ oz) cashews
- a large (adult) handful of ramps/wild garlic leaves
- ½ cup (50 g / 1¾ oz) grated Parmesan cheese
- 1 teaspoon lemon juice
- 2–3 pinches of salt
- 2 tablespoons olive oil (you may need to add a little more)

1. Wearing gloves, wash the nettles carefully in a colander.

2. Bring a pan of water to a boil over low heat and simmer the nettles for 2–3 minutes, ensuring all the nettles are submerged.

3. Drain the liquid—this makes a rather nice tea!

4. Dry the nettles off in a salad spinner or place in a tea towel and squeeze the liquid into a sink. You should end up with two adult-sized handfuls of nettle leaves.

5. Grind the cashews to a fine powder in a clean coffee grinder, seed grinder, or pestle and mortar. If you don't have any of these, try placing them in a sealed bag and bashing them with a rolling pin.

6. Put all the ingredients into a blender and whizz them for up to 5 seconds, adding a little more oil if required. If not fully blended, whizz for another 5 seconds or until it is a smooth paste. Serve with pasta.

LION'S TOOTH

The word dandelion comes from the French *dent-de-lion*, which translates as "tooth of lion" or "lion's tooth." The leaves are the shape of a spiky tooth, which also makes it easy to identify.

DANDELION *TARAXACUM* SPECIES

A very common plant with jagged, teeth-like leaves and yellow flowers giving way to a fluffy seed head. It generally grows as high as 6–8 in (15–20 cm), but can reach 10 in (25 cm) or more.

Other names
Dandelion clock, wet-the-bed, lion's tooth.

Leaves
2–10 in (5–25 cm) in length, the leaves grow from the base in what's known as a rosette formation. They are lobed or spiky.

Flowers
Bright yellow flowers, ¾–2 in (2–5 cm) in length, made up of what looks like hundreds of petals. After flowering, the fluffy, gray-white seed heads, like hundreds of umbrella skeletons, can be blown and dispersed in the wind.

Other characteristics
A hollow stem containing a white latex-like substance. A long brownish-white tap root.

What to avoid
Drooping or discolored plants may have been sprayed.

Where in the world?
Dandelions are found throughout North America and Europe.

Where to find it locally
Mostly on grassy areas. In wasteland, countryside, edges of woods and clearings, and hillsides.

HOW TO EAT IT

The whole of the dandelion plant can be eaten. The leaves are best eaten in the spring before the plant flowers (see "Bitterness" opposite). The roots can be eaten in the fall or early spring and cooked like a vegetable or roasted and ground into a drink, though they can be very bitter. The flower heads can be eaten in salads or cooked with sugar or honey to make a cordial or cough syrup. The flower buds are also edible, tasting best when blanched and served with butter or oil and a squeeze of lemon.

DANDELION FRITTATA

Ingredients

- 1 tablespoon wild ramps butter (page 36) or 1 tablespoon vegetable or olive oil
- $\frac{1}{2}$ red onion, finely chopped
- $\frac{1}{2}$ red pepper/bell pepper, finely chopped
- 2 garlic cloves (if using oil)
- $\frac{1}{2}$ cup (25 g / 1 oz) dandelion leaves, roughly chopped
- 6 eggs
- 3 tablespoons milk
- salt and pepper

1. Melt the butter or heat the oil in a pan over a moderate heat.

2. Add the chopped onion and pepper and cook until they start to soften (around 10–15 minutes). If you are using garlic cloves rather than wild garlic butter, add them after around 8 minutes.

3. Throw in the dandelion leaves and allow them to wilt.

4. In a bowl, beat the eggs, then add the milk. Sprinkle a little salt and pepper into the mix and pour it over the softened and wilted vegetables.

5. Once the underside of the frittata is browned, place the pan under a moderate grill until the egg stiffens and browns. Serve with a side salad.

BITTERNESS

Dandelion leaves can be quite bitter. They are less so in the spring and after heavy rain. However, if the bitterness is too much, try bringing the leaves to a boil at least twice and discard the water each time. Add other greens, such as nettles, and mix with melted butter, a squeeze of lemon and perhaps a dash of balsamic vinegar.

WILD RAMPS *ALLIUM TRICOCCUM* (USA);
WILD GARLIC, *ALLIUM URSINUM* (EUROPE)

A garlic-scented woodland plant with fat, pointed leaves and white flowers. Plants grow together in clumps, and it is not unusual to see a whole forest floor covered with ramps or wild garlic.

Other names
Ramp, ramson, wood leek, bear's garlic.

Leaves
Ramps leaves are typically ¾–2 in (2–5 cm) wide and can grow up to 16 in (40 cm) long. Wild garlic leaves tend to grow shorter, reaching around 6–8 in (15–20 cm) long. The leaves taper and form a point at the top, grow wide in the middle, and thin again at the bottom where they join the stalk.

Flowers
On a leafless stalk with a firework-like spray of flowers. Wild garlic has star-shaped flowers when the plant is still in leaf. Ramps have a small daisy-like flower borne after the leaves appear. The wild garlic plant does not have bell-shaped flowers, so avoid these.

Other characteristics
A strong, almost overpowering garlic smell. Ramps often have a red stem above the white spring-onion-like bulb, whereas wild garlic is green above ground with a white bulb. When foraging, dig up one bulb to positively identify the plant (but only one so they can reproduce); if there is no bulb, it is not wild garlic.

PROTECTED
Ramps are protected in Canada, and can also be in short supply elsewhere. Only ever harvest the leaves and leave the bulbs to allow more plants to grow.

Opposite Wild garlic, *Allium ursinum* (Europe).

Above Wild ramps, *Allium tricoccum* (USA).

What to avoid
If you can't smell onion or garlic then you have the wrong plant! Avoid plants with upright leaves or bell-shaped flowers. Take care not to mix with neighboring leaves of other plants; wash and check through the leaves when you get back home—break and smell any leaves that look different or you are uncertain of.

Where in the world?
In the Northeast and mountainous regions of eastern United States; in wooded areas of northern Europe.

Where to find it locally
Woodland, before the trees come into leaf. Ramps favor moist areas.

HOW TO EAT IT

Use the leaves in soups and stews, or make into a pesto, adding a milder leaf, such as nettle, to calm the fiery flavor (page 28). Leaves also add an extra flavor to curries or stir-fries. Or use in place of cloves of garlic.

WILD RAMPS BUTTER

Ingredients
- 2 cups (40 g / 1½ oz) ramps/wild garlic leaves
- 1 stick (125 g / 4½ oz) butter

1. Roll the ramps/wild garlic into a ball and chop into fine pieces. You may need to work over them with a knife a number of times as you want to be left with very small pieces of leaf (think tea-leaf-sized).

2. Soften the butter by squeezing it in your hands.

3. Using your hands, work the chopped leaves into the butter until it is all incorporated and evenly distributed. Shape into a log and wrap in foil.

WILD RAMPS BREAD

Ingredients
- a baguette
- wild ramps butter (see above)

1. Preheat the oven to 375°F (190°C).

2. At 1 in (2½ cm) intervals, cut into the bread—not all the way through, just down to the lower crust.

3. Add a teaspoon of wild ramps butter into each slice.

4. Wrap in aluminum foil and place on a baking tray and into the preheated oven.

5. Remove from the oven after 20 minutes; the bread should be crispy and all the garlic butter melted.

GOOSEFOOT *CHENOPODIUM ALBUM*

Shoots or small plants about 4 in (10 cm) appear in the spring, growing to 4–40 in (1/10–1 m) tall during the summer. Often found in small clumps, but solitary plants are not uncommon.

Other names
Fat hen, lamb's quarters, pigweed.

Leaves
Leaves are wavy, shaped like a goose's foot, in a triangle or diamond shape, wider closer to the plant and tapering to a point at the end. They are 2–5 in (5–12 cm) long and 1–4 in (3–10 cm) wide, lighter underneath than on top, often with a gray/white "dust." Leaves grow opposite each other.

Flowers
Goosefoot flowers throughout the summer, with dense clusters of green or red berry-shaped flowers around 1/16 in (2 mm) across. After flowering, on some species the green clusters open to reveal the seed, which will look like a little black or dark brown dot.

What to avoid
Avoid any leaves with very prominent veins and no gray/white coating.

Where in the world?
Very widespread across the United States and Europe in fertile soils.

Where to find it locally
A weed commonly found in vegetable gardens, farms, and community gardens, favoring ground which has just been dug or disturbed in some way.

HOW TO EAT IT

You can eat goosefoot raw, but only do so in moderation, just one or two leaves to try it. Otherwise, cook it and eat it as you would spinach. Try making a pesto, flavoring the mix with a few fresh basil leaves. The sprouted seeds can also be eaten. They need to be shaken from the plant first, then soaked overnight and washed thoroughly the next day.

WILTED GOOSEFOOT GREENS

Ingredients
- ⅛ cup (10 g / ¼ oz) sliced almonds
- 2 teaspoons olive oil
- ½ cup (50 g / 1¾ oz) goosefoot greens
- 1–2 tablespoons water
- ¼ teaspoon lemon juice
- pinch of salt

1. Toast the almonds in a dry pan until lightly browned. Set aside on a saucer or small plate.

2. Heat the oil in a pan over low heat, and once warmed, add the leaves and stir.

3. After about 30 seconds, add the water and continue to stir as the leaves wilt.

4. Add the lemon juice and sprinkle over the salt.

5. Add the toasted almonds and serve as a side dish.

AN ANCIENT PLANT

Fat hen, a cultivated form of goosefoot, is one of the oldest food plants in Europe and can often be found growing next to the ruins of ancient buildings. In the 1950s, the body of a man who died 2,400 years ago was found in a peat bog in Denmark. Along with barley, linseed, and sorrel, the seeds of fat hen were found in his stomach, meaning it is likely he had eaten them for his last meal in 400 BC.

CHICKWEED *STELLARIA MEDIA*

Chickweed is a small, common garden weed with white star-shaped flowers and pointed oval leaves. It can occasionally reach up to 2–12 in (5–30 cm), but usually forms a mat across the ground. The leaves grow on straggly, slightly hairy stalks, which grow from one central point. It is at its best in the spring, but you will find it all year round, although it tends to be less tasty in the summer months.

Leaves
Oval leaves growing opposite each other with long stalks, 1/10–3/4 in (3–20 mm). Leaves are close together on the top of the plant and more spread out closer to the base.

Flowers
Bright white star-shaped flowers with what look like ten petals (actually five sepals, five petals). It mostly flowers in the spring, but can flower at almost any time of the year.

Other characteristics
Chickweed is hairy on one side; this is much easier to see if you hold it up to light.

What to avoid
Plants with a white sap; plants with three veins on the leaf; and hairless plants.

Where in the world?
Very widespread throughout North America and Europe.

Where to find it locally
Parks and gardens, countryside and fields, and wasteland. It tends to like the base of trees or any bare ground it finds.

How to eat it
Harvest it with scissors. It works well in salads but has a mild flavor, so it is best mixed with stronger-tasting salad leaves such as wild arugula. Try experimenting by mixing it in with your favorite salad leaves.

MAKE A YUMMY DIP
Mix about 1 tablespoon of chopped chickweed (tops are best) with 3/4 cup (250 g / 9 oz) Greek yogurt, a 2 in (5 cm) chunk of cucumber cut into tiny pieces, a pinch of sumac powder (optional), and around 7–10 finely chopped mint leaves.

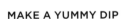

SPEARMINT *MENTHA SPICATA*

A square-stemmed plant with toothed leaves and a strong minty smell. Plants are usually between 1 ft (30 cm) and 1½–2 ft (45–60 cm) tall. It tends to grow in clumps. The roots spread out underneath the soil and quite often will pop up anywhere up to 3¼ ft (1 m) away from where they were planted.

Leaves
The leaves grow opposite each other on the plant stem. They are around 2 to 3½ in (5–9 cm) long.

Flowers
Spearmint flowers grow into long spikes of pinkish white flowers. Other kinds of mint have similar-colored flowers, but they are more like a series of pom-poms growing up from an elongated stem.

Other characteristics
There are many kinds of mint, all of which are edible. All plants in the mint family have a square stem. The only other plants with square stems are figworts (which don't smell of mint) and nettles, which have stinging hairs. In short, if it has a square stem and smells of mint, it most likely *is* mint!

Where in the world?
Spearmint is common in the United States and southern Canada. It is found throughout Europe, but is scarce in Ireland (where water mint is common).

Where to find it locally
Mint prefers moist areas; it also escapes from gardens quite easily so you often find it close to houses.

HOW TO EAT IT

Pour boiling water onto a handful of leaves to make mint tea, or blend a handful with a large slice of watermelon to make a refreshing drink. Try it with Greek yogurt (see chickweed dip, page 42) or sparingly in a salad with cucumber and feta cheese.

NETTLE AND MINT SMOOTHIE

This makes enough for two really yummy green smoothies. It is packed with enough goodness to keep grown-ups from constantly complaining that you don't eat enough healthy food.

Ingredients

- ½ avocado
- ½ cup (75 g / 2¾ oz) cucumber
- 1 ripe banana
- 1¼ cups (300 ml / 10 fl oz) of your favorite milk*
- 1½ cups (50 g / 1¾ oz) nettles or spinach, stalks removed (wear gloves when removing stalks)
- 3 tablespoons mint leaves
- 1 teaspoon maple syrup or birch syrup (page 139, optional)
- juice of 1½ limes

*This works well with cow's milk, but you can also use cashew milk, almond milk or any other plant-based milks.

1. Put the avocado, cucumber, and banana into a blender. Add the milk, turn on the blender, and whizz for 5 seconds.

2. Add the nettles or spinach, the mint, and the maple or birch syrup, if using, and whizz for 5 seconds again.

3. Squeeze in the lime juice and whizz for 2 seconds.

MINT ICE CUBES

Carefully place one or two mint leaves into each section of an ice-cube tray and top with water. Put the tray in the freezer and wait for six hours. Goes well with lemonade (see sumac lemonade, page 126).

GARLIC MUSTARD *ALLIARIA PETIOLATA*

In the first year it is a low-lying plant with rounded, heart-shaped leaves growing in a rosette (from one central point). In its second year it has white flowers and reaches between 1 ft (30 cm) to 3 ft (1 m) in height.

Other names
Jack-by-the-hedge.

Leaves
Leaves are heart shaped with toothed edges and prominent veins. They have a rounded tip in young plants and a pointed tip in older, flowering plants. Most leaves are 2–4 in (5–10 cm) across, but can grow much larger in fertile soil.

Flowers
Flowers appear in the spring, with four petals measuring ⅓ –⅔ in (1–1½ cm) across. They are white and cross shaped, and cluster together at the tip of the plant. Immature flowers look a lot like a sprouting broccoli.

Other characteristics
It has long, thin pods, around 1–2½ in (2½–6 cm) long, which form as the plant flowers then mature to contain seeds. The seeds are diamond shaped and taste of mustard. The plant has a garlic-like smell, especially when the leaves are crushed. The stems are very hairy at the base, becoming hairless at the top. The leaf stems can also be hairy.

What to avoid
Avoid any plant that doesn't have a garlic-like smell when crushed, or a garlic-like taste when eaten. Also avoid plants with purple or yellow flowers, or those which are hairy all the way up. Look for the flowering plant to ID the plant for the first time, then harvest

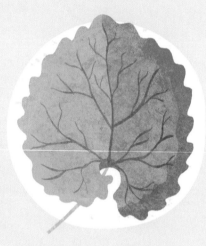

leaves from plants which have not flowered as they are better to eat.

Where in the world?
It has been introduced to the northwestern, midwestern, and most of the eastern United States as well as Canada. It is also found all over Europe.

Where to find it locally
Grows best in the shade, along hedgerows, the edges of woods, roadsides, lanes, and neglected corners of parks and gardens.

HOW TO EAT IT

Pick the leaves before they flower. They have a garlic- and mustard-like taste and can be used in salads, in pesto, or to flavor soups and stews. The immature flowers can be cooked like broccoli (they are more bitter), and the roots can be used like horseradish.

JUMPING JACK WRAPS

Ingredients

- 20–30 garlic mustard leaves (from first-year plant/before it has flowered)
- ½ cup (100 g / 3½ oz) couscous
- ¾ cup (185 ml / 6 fl oz) vegetable stock
- handful of fresh parsley, finely chopped
- 1 teaspoon fresh thyme, finely chopped
- 1 tablespoon raisins
- 1 tablespoon pine nuts
- 1 tablespoon lemon juice

1. Blanch the garlic mustard leaves in a pan of boiling water for 3–4 minutes, remove with a slotted spoon, then dunk in cold water and pat each one dry with a paper towel.

2. In a large bowl, cover the couscous with the freshly boiled stock. Cover the bowl with a plate and leave for 5–6 minutes, or until all the liquid has been absorbed, then fluff the couscous with a spoon.

3. Stir in the herbs, followed by the remaining ingredients.

4. Place a teaspoon-sized amount of the mixture in the center of each leaf. Fold the sides in and roll like a burrito. Serve as a side or snack.

PLANTAIN *PLANTAGO MAJOR*

A small plant, about 6–12 in (15–30 cm) across, with a long flowering spike and ribbed leaves growing out from a central point. They mostly grow on compacted ground in small clumps. The leaves grow out from a central point in what is known as a rosette formation. Not to be confused with plantain bananas; same name, very different plant!

Other names
Groblad, white man's foot.

Leaves
The leaves are oval-shaped, 2–8 in (5–20 cm) long and 1½–3½ in (4–9 cm) wide (sometimes bigger), with rib-like veins running from the base (at the stem) to the top of the leaf.

Flowers
The flower is made up of a cluster of small flowers on a long spike (up to 6 in / 15 cm), which rises up from the center of the plant. These go to seed very quickly and you are left with a large spike covered in tiny black seeds.

Where in the world?
Found in the eastern and western United States, southern Canada, and throughout Europe.

Where to find it locally
Grassy areas, especially on land which has been compacted. It is sometimes called "white man's foot" as the seeds were said to have been dispersed by the incoming settlers in America.

OTHER SPECIES
There are many other edible plantains, including ribwort (*Plantago lanceolata*), which has spear-shaped leaves, and buck's horn plantain (*Plantago coronopus*), which has antler-shaped leaves and grows by the sea.

How to eat it
Toast the mature seed heads (brown not green) on a campfire, then pull the seeds off with your teeth; they taste like rye crackers. Pick leaves from small, younger plants; they have quite a mushroom-like taste. If you find raw leaves too bitter, cook for about 2 minutes in boiling water, then fry them up in some butter. Just as with common foods such as beans, eggs, and those containing gluten, a small minority of people can be allergic to plantain, so only eat a small amount the first time you try the plant.

SUMMER

After the spring blossom comes
the summer fruit. Look for bushes
brimming with blackberries,
wild blueberries, and elderberries.

WILD CHERRY *PRUNUS AVIUM*

A commonly found tree with white blossom and round red or purplish-black fruit with a long stalk and a single pit. Domestic cherry trees usually only grow to 11½–15 ft (3½–4½ m), but wild cherry trees can grow up to 100 ft (30 m). The width of the spread of their branches is normally equal to their height. More often than not, cherries grow into trees, but sometimes you see the branches spread out like a fan across a garden wall. Occasionally they may also be cut into a hedge on the edge of a field or garden. However, it is quite common to see them planted in rows, especially in urban areas, so you will often find more than one at a time.

Leaves
The leaves are long, 2–6 in (6–15 cm), oval shaped, and dark green with pointed tips and toothed edges. The veins run at a slight angle from the center at regular intervals.

Blossom
Wild cherries have white or pinkish white blossom with five petals.

Fruit
Cherries grow in clusters on single stalks; they never grow on vines like tomatoes or grapes. Where the cherry meets the stalk it is curved inwards like a crater. The color ranges from bright red to purple/black, but never totally black. They have a single pit. Take a look at supermarket cherries before you head out foraging if you are unsure what they look like.

CHERRY LEAVES
Red pimples or glands on the leaf stalk produce nectar and attract insects that will protect the tree from predators.

What to avoid
Buckthorn has overly curved veins on the leaves and black fruit; they also have thorns. Cherry laurel has glossy, waxy leaves, with many fruits growing on a single stem. Avoid the smaller bitter bird cherries (*Prunus padus*).

regions of the United States, as well as throughout Europe.

Where in the world?
Wild cherries are mostly found in northwest, northeast, and central

Where to find it locally
Parks and gardens, roadside, old orchards, edgeland.

HOW TO EAT IT

Cherries are best eaten straight from the tree. All cherries make excellent jams. Sour cherries (*Prunus cerasus*) are best for cooking and make excellent cherry pies.

CHERRY ICE POPS

Ingredients

- 1 medium banana
- 2 tablespoons natural yogurt
- 1½ cups (200 g / 7 oz) wild cherries
- 2 tablespoons fresh orange juice

1. Blend the banana and yogurt in a blender or smoothie maker.

2. Remove the cherry pits and add the cherries to the blender, then slowly add the orange juice and whizz.

3. Pour into ice pop molds and freeze for at least 6 hours.

4. If the ice pops are stuck in the molds as you remove them, run some warm (but not too hot) water over them.

BITTER VS SOUR

The smaller bird cherries (*Prunus padus*) can taste very bitter while the sour cherries (*Prunus cerasus*) live up to their name and taste very sour. The bitter-tasting bird cherries should be avoided as they can cause a stomachache.

ELDER *SAMBUCUS NIGRA*

The elder "tree" is a flowering shrub which grows to around 20 ft (6 m) in height, though it can grow taller than this, up to 49 ft (15 m). It produces heads of creamy-white flowers in the spring and dark purple or reddish-black berries. Both the berries and the flowers are only edible once cooked.

Leaves
The leaf is made up of five to seven leaflets or small leaves. Each leaflet is a long oval shape which grows opposite another. The leaflets have prominent veins and serrated edges.

Flowers
Umbels or an umbrella-like spray of white flowers on a single stalk. Each single flower is around ¼ in (5 mm) and the whole umbel or cluster is around 8 in (20 cm) across.

Fruit
Lots of small purple or blackish fruits which squish very easily. Like the flowers, they have an umbrella-like spread to them. The stem turns purplish red when the fruit ripens and the berries droop downwards.

Branches
The branches have lots of bumpy spots, and if you cut into a branch it gives off a very distinctive smell.

What to avoid
Avoid anything with thorns. Also avoid dwarf elder (*Sambucus ebulus*), which grows on a single, non-woody stem, has long flame-shaped leaflets and berries which stand upright rather than drooping down. Also avoid pokeberry, which has a long strand of fruit on a single stem. Elderberries always droop downwards in an umbel or umbrella-shaped formation.

Opposite The berries are small purple or blackish fruits, with an umbrella-like spread to them.

Left To spot elderflowers, look for an umbrella-like spray of white flowers on a single stalk.

Where in the world?

Common throughout Europe with the exception of northern Scandinavia and southwest Spain. A closely related subspecies of *Sambucus nigra* grows throughout North America. The American elder *Sambucus canadensis* can also be found in the eastern United States, eastern Canada, and California.

Where to find it locally

Grows in hedgerows and on wasteland. Also found in parks and gardens and on the edge of forests.

HOW TO EAT IT

The stems and berries contain a poisonous substance called cyanide, which is thankfully destroyed by cooking. For this reason, you should never eat raw elderberries! The flowers can be dipped in batter and deep-fried to make elderflower fritters (always deep-fry with a responsible adult). A simple summer drink to make is elderflower cordial; you'll find countless recipes for this on the internet and in cookery books. It will keep for around a month, or you can store it in plastic bottles and freeze it to store for longer—be sure to leave a gap at the top of the bottle to allow the frozen liquid to expand.

ELDERBERRY SYRUP

Ingredients
- ⅔ cup (100 g / 3½ oz) fresh elderberries
- 1¾ cups (400 ml / 14 fl oz) water
- 3 dried cloves
- 1 in (2½ cm) piece of fresh ginger
- ½ teaspoon cinnamon
- scant ½ cup (100 ml / 3½ fl oz) honey
- ½ cup (100 g / 3½ oz) granulated sugar

1. In a large pan, bring all the ingredients except the honey and sugar to a rolling boil.

2. Pour the mixture into a slow cooker set to medium for 1½ to 2 hours, or simmer over low heat for 45 minutes to an hour, or until the mixture is reduced by half.

3. Remove from the slow cooker or stovetop, pour through a sieve into a pan, and add the honey and sugar, stirring until dissolved. If necessary, reheat the mix to dissolve the honey and sugar.

4. Allow to cool and place the contents in a clean, sterilized jar.

5. Use 1–2 teaspoons at a time as a syrup, or add water and drink as a cordial.

ELDER SHORTBREAD

Ingredients

- 2 tablespoons fresh elderflowers
- 1 stick (100 g / 3½ oz) butter or vegan margarine
- ¼ cup (50 g / 2 oz) granulated sugar
- 1 cup (150 g / 5 oz) all-purpose flour

1. Preheat the oven to 350°F (180°C).

2. Using your fingers, remove the elderflowers from their stems, place them in a large bowl, and set aside. It is important to remove as much of the stalk as possible. However, there is no need to worry if tiny pieces of stalk end up in the bowl as it is impossible to remove it all.

3. Cut the butter into cubes and place this in a separate bowl along with the remaining ingredients.

4. Using your fingers again, rub the ingredients together so they start to look like breadcrumbs or an apple crumble topping.

5. Add the elderflowers and roughly mix everything together.

6. Push the crumb mix together with your hands so it forms a dough, then push this down into a greased baking tin.

7. Bake for 20 minutes, until golden.

WILD BLUEBERRY

VACCINIUM ANGUSTIFOLIUM (USA);
BILBERRY, *VACCINIUM MYRTILLUS* (EUROPE)

Wild blueberries and bilberries are part of the genus *Vaccinium*, which also includes the red cranberry and the highbush blueberry (see "Highbush Blueberry," page 67). Wild blueberries and bilberries are around 4–23½ in (10–60 cm) high.

Other names
Whortleberry, low-bush blueberry.

Leaves
The leaves can be very finely toothed (although not in all species), pointed at both ends, and either long and thin or egg shaped. They are normally between ¾–1½ in (2–4 cm) long, and they change color at the end of the season.

Flowers
Flowers arrive in the late spring. They are white to pink, sometimes a light red, and bell or blueberry shaped.

Fruit
Fruit is ready in mid to late summer; the berries will stain your fingers purple. They are round and dark blue with a violet or purple tinge to them and ⅛–⅓ in (½–1 cm) in diameter. Bilberries have a circle-shaped calyx at the bottom of the fruit, and blueberries a crown-shaped calyx.

What to avoid
Avoid any berry with a separate calyx attaching it to the plant (as with a strawberry or tomato). Also avoid plants where the fruit sticks upwards or clusters together on a stem (see pokeberry, page 60), and always avoid any fruits which *do not* stain your fingers purple.

WHAT IS A CALYX?
It is a structure which forms to protect the flower. As the flower grows into the fruit, the calyx often stays; on a strawberry or tomato it is the green part you remove before eating. Wild blueberries/bilberries have no calyx; instead they have a crown or ring.

Opposite Bilberry, *Vaccinium myrtillus* (Europe).

Above Wild blueberry, *Vaccinium angustifolium* (USA).

Where in the world?

Vaccinium angustifolium found in the eastern United States; *Vaccinium myrtillus* found across Europe.

Where to find it locally

Wild blueberries and bilberries grow on moors and heathland. They can also be found on the edges of woods and in woodland clearings.

HOW TO EAT IT

Wild blueberries and bilberries can be picked by hand or using a berry picker. They can be eaten straight from the plant or put into a tub and taken home. They freeze very well. They can be made into jams, added to ice cream, put on breakfast cereals, or added to smoothies.

WILD BLUEBERRY FLAPJACK

Ingredients

- 6 tablespoons (80 g / 3 oz) butter
- 3 tablespoons honey
- 3 tablespoons apple juice concentrate (ask in health food stores)
- 2 cups (180 g / 6 oz) oats
- 1 cup (100 g / 3½ oz) wild blueberries or bilberries

This makes one small pan (approx. 7 x 11 in/18 x 28 cm), but you can double the mix if you find more berries.

1. Preheat the oven to 375°F (190°C).

2. Melt the butter in a pan over low heat.

3. Add the honey and apple juice concentrate.

4. Stir in the oats.

5. Once the oats have soaked up the butter mix, gradually stir in the berries, a few at a time.

6. Press the flapjack mix into a greased baking tray.

7. Bake for 20–25 minutes, or until the flapjacks are golden brown.

8. Cool and serve, or use for packed lunches.

HIGHBUSH BLUEBERRY

The highbush blueberry (*Vaccinium corymbosum*) is a plant native to the wet woodlands of the eastern United States and Canada. Its fruit is much larger than the wild blueberry, and much more like the blueberry you find in your local store. It is a cross between the two plants.

VIRGINIA GLASSWORT *SALICORNIA DEPRESSA* (USA)*;* MARSH SAMPHIRE, *SALICORNIA EUROPAEA* (EUROPE)

A very distinctive little plant, resembling a miniature, spineless cactus. It measures up to 1 ft (30 cm) high, but many are far shorter, measuring just 6 in (15 cm).

Other names
Glasswort, American glasswort.

Leaves
No leaves to speak of; instead it has a segmented stem or stalk with lots of bumpy branches.

Flowers
It is rare to see the flowers, which are tiny yellow dots less than $1/24$ in (1 mm) and grow over the stem of the plant.

Where in the world?
All over North America and coastal Europe.

FISHMONGERS
Marsh samphire is traditionally sold in fishmongers in Europe; find some for sale to help identify it in the wild.

IMPORTANT NOTE
It is very easy to get stuck in the mud when picking glasswort. It is a great excuse to go barefoot and get really muddy, but it is also best to keep a grown-up nearby to pull you out, should you get stuck!

Opposite Marsh samphire, *Salicornia europaea*, grows across Europe in salt marshes.

Above American or Virginia glasswort, *Salicornia depressa*; sometimes *Salicornia virginica*, is found in salt marshes of California and elsewhere in North America.

Where to find it locally

It can be found in the marsh flats of tidal salt marshes. Look for it in the mud when the tide goes out, but be sure to check the tide times and give yourself plenty of time to escape the sea as it washes back in.

How to eat it

Glasswort is very salty so it doesn't need any seasoning. It is best to cook it to get rid of any nasties it may have taken up as it was growing. Place it in a pan of boiling water for about 2 minutes (or for just 30 seconds if you like it crunchy). Try it with a squeeze of lemon juice and a little olive oil or melted butter.

SHEEP'S SORREL

RUMEX ACETOSELLA (USA);

COMMON SORREL, *RUMEX ACETOSA* (EUROPE)

Grows up to 2–3 ft (60–100 cm) high, with each clump spreading to 1–3 ft (30–100 cm), mostly in grassland and meadows. When it goes to flower in the summer, from a distance you will see flecks of red among the long grass. It has arrow-shaped leaves, which can look a little like dock leaves.

Leaves

The leaves are light green and arrow shaped. Appearing in a rosette or round clump, they measure 4–6 in (10–15 cm) in length, sometimes more. In extreme conditions, such as on moorland, you can find leaves as little as $\frac{1}{3}$ in (1 cm) in length. It is important to look for the veins in the leaf; these run from the center to the outer edge.

Flowers

The flowers are almost too small to see; they are red, cup shaped, grow on a stalk, and only measure about $\frac{1}{12}$ in (2 mm) across.

Fruit

Sorrel "fruit" is a flat, reddish pink papery case with a single seed in the middle. It comes after the flower on a long shoot. The fruit turns darker as it develops, and the plant will produce many tiny brown seeds.

What to avoid

Lords and ladies (*Arum maculatum*) can look like sorrel. They have arrow-shaped leaves which grow in the shade, and one continuous vein running around the inner margin of the leaf. In the later spring they have a flower which looks like a peace lily, and in the summer they have a spike of orange-red berries the size of peas. To best avoid this plant, only pick plants in open, shade-free locations, and to begin with only look for sorrel in the early summer onwards.

Where in the world?

Sheep's sorrel is found in the United States, Canada, and Europe. Common sorrel is found throughout Europe.

Where to find it locally

Sorrel is most common in grassland and meadows where the soil is slightly damp, although if an area is prone to flooding it will disappear. You can also find it by the side of roads and paths, in gardens, and on wasteland.

Opposite Common sorrel, *Rumex acetosa* (Europe).

Above Sheep's sorrel, *Rumex acetosella* (USA).

HOW TO EAT IT

Sorrel can be a welcome nibble when you are out walking. It is good in salads or wilted down with a bit of butter (most leaves are) alongside fish, especially salmon and trout.

YOGURT AND SORREL DIPPING SAUCE

Ingredients

- ¼ cup (25–30 g / 1 oz) sorrel leaves
- ¾ cup (250 g / 9 oz) Greek yogurt
- ⅓ cup (80 ml / 3 fl oz) olive oil
- a pinch of salt and a twist of ground black pepper

1. Give the sorrel leaves a good wash and chop them as finely as possible.

2. Mix the chopped leaves in with the yogurt.

3. Slowly add the oil, stirring all the time. Season with salt and pepper to taste.

4. Serve as a side to fish, falafel, or the sweet potato and chestnut burgers (page 123). Also makes a good dipping sauce for carrot sticks or chips.

HINT OF LEMON

The lemony flavor of sorrel comes from a substance called oxalic acid. The same substance is present in wood sorrel, giving it that same distinctive sharp taste. Oxalic acid can also be found in rhubarb, spinach, beets, and peanuts. Eating foods high in oxalic acid can cause kidney stones in those who are prone to this condition. Drinking plenty of water helps flush it out of the body before it can do any harm.

GIANT PUFFBALL *CALVATIA GIGANTEA*

Puffballs are practically unmistakable: they are large, ball-shaped mushrooms, which can grow to the size of a basketball or even bigger! Yet despite their size and shape, they can be hard to find. It is easy to get excited when you think you have found one growing, only to get closer and find out it is a soccer ball or a plastic bag.

Shape
Puffballs are irregularly shaped, but can be seen as roughly ball shaped, or like an egg or a football on its side. They have a smooth skin which some say feels a little like suede.

Size
Their size can range between that of a grapefruit and a soccer ball.

What to avoid
Some poisonous mushrooms can look like puffballs, but it is possible to distinguish by cutting into them. A poisonous mushroom will look like a mushroom within a mushroom (see inset picture, opposite), whereas a puffball's flesh is a constant and unbroken white all the way through. Puffballs also have no stalk.

Before you pick
Cut a small piece of the puffball before you pick it. If it has gone yellow or brown inside, this means it is no longer ripe and you should leave it as it will spore, which will make more yummy puffballs for the following year.

Where in the world?
Puffballs can be found throughout either temperate or cool-weather places in North America and Europe. They are protected in parts of Europe such as Poland, Lithuania, and Norway.

Where to find it locally
Puffballs grow on grassland and by the sides of roads, often near nettles. They are very hard to find, so rather than setting out specifically to look for one, just keep your eyes peeled whenever you are out and about.

HOW TO EAT IT

Puffballs have quite a mild flavor and can be used in place of tofu in stir-fries. They can be cut into cubes, fried in butter and served on toast with a little parsley. Or make them into burgers by cutting them into burger shapes and grilling or frying until they are golden brown and cooked through. They can be served in a bun with a salad and relish of your choice.

PUFFBALL KEBABS

Depending on the size of the skewer, you will need 8-12 chunks/cubes of vegetables for each kebab: 1 zucchini, 1 bell pepper, 8-16 cherry tomatoes, 1 onion, and 1 puffball should easily be enough for 8 small skewers.

Ingredients
- any of the following vegetables:
  – bell peppers
  – zucchini
  – cherry tomatoes
  – red onions
- 1 giant puffball mushroom
- halloumi cheese
- a little olive oil

1. Cut the vegetables, puffball, and cheese into 1 in (2-3 cm) pieces. It is unlikely you will need the whole puffball, so cut it in half and use what you need.

2. Push all the cubes onto skewers in an even distribution.

3. Coat in olive oil and cook on the barbecue, turning so they do not burn—young children may need to get their grown-up to do this.

Finley O'Neill, a schoolboy from Slaithwaite in West Yorkshire, UK, holds the world record for the largest puffball ever found. It measured nearly 5 ft 7 in ($1^3/_4$ m) across and weighed 35 lb (16 kg).

WILD RADISH *RAPHANUS RAPHANISTRUM*

A leafy plant, 19½–47 in (50–120 cm) tall (sometimes taller) with yellow, white, or lilac cross-shaped flowers.

Leaves
The leaves form a rosette, which means they spread out from a central point (carrots do the same), 2–15½ in (5–40 cm) long and ¾–6 in (2–15 cm) wide. The leaves are lobed, meaning they are made of many lobes (think of the shape of an ear lobe) on either side of the stem. They tend to die back when the plant is in fruit or going to seed.

Flowers
Four petals in a cross shape, ⅓–¾ in (1–2 cm) long. Flowers can be yellow, white, or sometimes lilac. They have a very noticeable vein running down the center of the petal. The sepals (the cup-like casing around the petals) are ⅛–⅓ in (½–1 cm) long and can be purple if the flowers are white and yellow, or green for yellow flowers, sometimes with a purple tinge at the base of the sepal near the stem.

Fruit
The fruit pods are very distinctive. They are ribbed or bumpy, a little like two, three, or four small green balls stacked on top of each other. On the top "ball" there is a long pointy spike. Sea rocket looks similar with a thinner fruit, and is also edible.

Other ways to identify it
When the plant goes to flower, it sends up a branched stem with tiny leaves on and the flowers or fruit perched on the end. Crushed leaves give off a radish- or mustard-like scent.

DID YOU KNOW?
Wild radish is a cruciferous plant, from the Latin *crux* meaning "cross," referring to the cross-shaped flowers.

Where in the world?
Common throughout North America and Europe.

Where to find it locally
It can be found on farmland, edgeland or where the soil has been recently dug or disturbed. Its closely related relative *Raphanus raphanistrum* ssp. *maritimus*, or sea radish, is found by the coast. Garden radishes also produce an edible seed pod if left to go to seed.

How to eat it
The leaves are very spicy, like a mustard or strong salad arugula. The seed pods are much milder and make an excellent snack, although they only have a short season before they go hard and become inedible. Gently bite down on a seed pod to test the ripeness; if it is at all hard it has gone over and cannot be eaten.

Opposite Wild radish flowers feature four petals in a cross shape. They can be white, pink, or yellow.

Above The fruit pods look like several small green balls stacked on top of each other, with a long pointy spike on one end.

Main image Woodland strawberry, *Fragaria vesca* (Europe). **Inset** Virginian strawberry, *Fragaria virginiana* (USA)

VIRGINIAN STRAWBERRY

FRAGARIA VIRGINIANA (USA);
WOODLAND STRAWBERRY, *FRAGARIA VESCA* (EUROPE)

A tiny plant, with even tinier red fruit, and often easy to miss. Grows to
about 1 ft (30 cm) tall and spreads to about the same width.

Other names
Wild strawberry, alpine strawberry.

Leaves
Three leaves, two opposite each other and one
on top. Dark green with serrated or toothed edges.

Flowers
Small white flowers $1/3$–$2/3$ in (1–$1^1/2$ cm) with five petals.

Fruit
About $2/3$ in ($1^1/2$ cm) in diameter. Red with seeds on the outside, like
a regular strawberry in miniature. They are white before they ripen.

Other ways to identify it
Just like spider plants or regular strawberries, wild strawberries send out
"runners." These are tiny clones or copies of the adult plant on long stalks,
up to $6^1/2$ ft (2 m) long.

Lookalikes
The mock strawberry (*Duchesnea indica*) has much rounder fruits and yellow flowers
and can be found mostly in churchyards and gardens. It is a cruel lookalike as it
tastes almost of nothing!

Where in the world?
Widespread in North
America and Europe.

Where to find it locally
Likes dry conditions in
woodlands. It is also found
by the side of paths, on
roadsides, and in hedges.
Look for the flowers in the
spring first, then come
back for the fruit.

HOW TO EAT IT

They are so tasty and small, it is rare that you will ever make it home with your wild strawberries. Best eaten with two hands, one hand putting the fruit in your mouth and the other reaching for the next one. If you do manage to get them home, they are good with ice cream or mixed with other fruit and a little juice as a fruit salad. You could use the larger strawberries in any recipe (although I wouldn't make jam with them—you'll spend all day picking enough to make it worthwhile).

WILD STRAWBERRY CRANACHAN

Ingredients
- 200 g / 7 oz Wild Blueberry Flapjack (page 66)
- 1 cup (240 g / 8½ oz) Greek or thick yogurt
- 1 cup (200 g / 7 oz) strawberries (or mixed soft fruit)

For a double taste of wild strawberries, make the flapjacks with these rather than blueberries or bilberries.

1. Crumble up the flapjack and layer it in the bottom of two large or four small glasses.

2. Add a layer of yogurt.

3. Chop the fruit and add a little to the yogurt.

4. Repeat steps 2 and 3 until the glasses are full.

Our modern strawberries are the result of a cross between a type of European wild strawberry and a strawberry from Chile. Before the seventeenth century, the large strawberries you buy in the supermarket did not exist!

WILD PLUM *PRUNUS DOMESTICA*

A small tree growing between 8–13 ft (2½ and 4 m) tall, with white blossom and, depending on the variety, red, purple, yellow, or green fruit. It has a light brown to grayish, slightly cracked trunk lacking the broken lines of a cherry. Unlike some American varieties, the European wild plum has no thorns.

Other names
European wild plum (damson, bullace, greengage are varieties).

Leaves
Quite large leaves, up to 2–4 in (5–10 cm) long and 1–2 in (2½–5 cm) wide. They are oval shaped and go to a point at the top end and into the hairy leaf stem at the bottom. They have small "teeth" around the edges.

Flowers
Look for five-petaled, round-ended (not split-ended) white blossom (flowers), about ¾ in (2 cm) in diameter with long stamens in the spring. Unlike the sloe (see below), the blossom comes at the same time as the leaves.

Fruit
The fruit has a single flattened seed or pit, which is easy to remove. They are oval to egg shaped and have a groove running down one side. Plums can be purple, red, yellow or green and around 2½ in (6 cm) long, and can have a harmless powdery coating which is easy to rub off. Damsons and bullaces are a little smaller than plums and come less easily from the pit. Both can be quite sharp and are better for cooking. Sloes are even smaller still, about the size of a grape, and have long thorns on their branches. Sloes are very astringent (they dry out your mouth) and not very pleasant to eat raw. If you find them, give them to a grown-up, tell them it's a small juicy plum, and watch their reaction!

Where in the world?
Plums are common across North America and Europe. *Prunus domestica* can be found in western and northeastern parts of the United States and across Europe. The American wild plum (*Prunus americana*), with its large yellow, sweet fruit, and the Chickasaw or Cherokee plum (*Prunus angustifolia*), with its large cherry-like fruits are more common in the eastern United States.

Where to find it locally
You will quite often see the plum growing in hedgerows and on the edges of woods, along with gardens, parks, and on wasteland.

HOW TO EAT IT

Sweet varieties are best eaten raw off the tree; cook the tarter fruits in pies and jams.

PLUMS IN HONEY AND THYME

Ingredients
- 8 ripe plums cut in two, pits removed (or enough to fill a baking tray)
- a little honey
- a few sprigs of thyme

1. Preheat the oven to 375°F (190°C).

2. Put the plums on the baking tray with the skin facing down.

3. Fill the hole where the plum pit was with honey.

4. Bake for 10 minutes, then remove from the oven and sprinkle over the sprigs of thyme.

5. Place back in the oven and bake for another 5–10 minutes, or until the plums are soft and the honey has started to brown.

OTHER KINDS OF PLUM

All plums have fruits with a single seed and a five-petaled, white blossom (flower) in spring. Cherry plum (*Prunus cerasifera*) is native to southern Europe, but can be found across Britain and can occasionally be seen in North America. It has delicious purple, red or yellow fruits slightly larger than a cherry. Beech plum (*Prunus maritima*), another edible plum, is found on dunes in the northeastern United States and southeastern coast of Canada. The edible fruit is light purple, green, yellow, reddish, and (rarely) blue.

BLACKBERRY *RUBUS FRUTICOSUS*

Blackberries are found on a tangled, thorny shrub which grows into a thick bush up to 10 ft (3 m) high. In Europe, blackberries are also known as brambles. In the United States, however, a bramble can refer to a raspberry or a blackberry. Raspberries are red and have a hollow inside, as the stalk stays on the plant. Blackberries are black and have a central stalk, which remains on the fruit.

Leaves
The leaves are toothed or jagged around the edge and come in groups of three or five, with the largest leaf at the top in the middle. The veins of the leaves can be prickly.

Flowers
The flowers are white or whitish pink with five petals. As a member of the rose family, they can look like a wild rose or apple blossom.

Fruit
As the fruit ripens it turns from green to red to black when it is ready. Each fruit is made up of lots of much smaller spheres called "drupes."

Where in the world?
On the eastern seaboard and west coast of the United States; all over the United Kingdom and northern Europe.

Where to find it locally
Blackberries are sometimes grown intentionally in gardens, but they are also a very common weed. They naturally grow on the edges of woods, but they also grow in neglected places such as empty building plots, parks, and overgrown gardens.

HOW TO EAT IT

Blackberries can be eaten raw or made into jam. The sweetest blackberry is always the first one to ripen on the tip of the growing stalk. I used to tell my brother that these were the ones with the most maggots; he always left them to me after that. You can freeze blackberries when they are in season to give you a supply during the winter. To avoid them sticking together, freeze them first on a tray with a gap between each berry; once frozen, transfer to a sealable container such as a recycled plastic takeout container. Early in the season, before the thorns develop, the shoots of a blackberry plant can be eaten; they taste a bit like butter.

BLACKBERRY CHEESECAKE

Ingredients

- 1½ cups (120 g / 4 oz) graham crackers (or you can use spice cookies)
- ¼ cup (60 g / 2 oz) butter, melted
- any 2 of the following (totaling 8 tablespoons): Greek yogurt; heavy cream, whipped; mascarpone cheese; cream cheese
- ⅓ cup (50 g / 2 oz) blackberries, chopped (leave a few whole, to decorate)

This is quite a versatile recipe as you can adapt it to whatever you have in the refrigerator or pantry. You can also make it with raspberries, strawberries, or wild blueberries.

1. Bash the graham crackers in a sealed bag with a rolling pin until they have turned to crumbs.

2. Put the crumbs in a heatproof bowl and mix in the melted butter.

3. Press the butter and graham cracker base down into four individual ramekins or one small 6 in (15 cm) tart pan. Once cool, chill in the refrigerator for at least 30 minutes.

4. Mix your two chosen (white) ingredients together in a bowl.

5. Add the blackberries to the white ingredients and stir to combine.

6. Add the creamy mix to the base and smooth the top down with the back of a spoon.

7. Add a few blackberries on top for decoration.

8. Put into the refrigerator for 1 hour.

FALL

As the nights draw in there is
comfort food aplenty with sweet
chestnuts, hazelnuts, and beech
nuts all falling from the trees.

APPLE _MALUS x DOMESTICA_

A common tree ranging from around 6½–33 ft (2–10 m) tall with white to pink blossom and distinctive red to green fruits.

Leaves
Leaves are oval shaped with toothed edges. They are dark green and can be slightly woolly or furry underneath.

Blossom
Spring blossom flowers can be pink when closed and white or whitish pink when open. They have five petals and long stamens.

Fruit
Apples are one of the most widely eaten and common fruits in the world. It is almost impossible to mistake full-size fruit for anything else, other than perhaps an equally edible pear or smaller crab apple. The fruits are green, red, or somewhere in between, about the size of a tennis ball or smaller, and appear on a single stalk rather than in clusters.

Where in the world?
In most of North America and across Europe.

Where to find it locally
Apples can be found in older orchards, parks, gardens, on wasteland or edgeland, and often in hedgerows. They grow from discarded seeds and are often found by the side of the road or rail lines (pick from both these locations with care).

HOW TO EAT IT

Apples can be eaten raw or cooked, and can store very well. Wild apples can be a gamble, tasting anything from delicious and juicy to bland and potato like. Some are so tart they remove all the moisture from your mouth. Try adding maple syrup, sugar, or honey to tart apples to sweeten them up.

APPLE SAUCE

Ingredients

The amount of sauce this makes will depend on the size and number of apples you use, but 5 medium to large (750 g / 1 lb 10 oz) apples makes about 2 cups (500 ml / 18 fl oz) of sauce.

1. Wash, peel, core and chop the apples.

2. Put the apples in a pan, adding about 1/2 cup (120 ml / 4 fl oz) of water for every five apples.

3. Place the pan over low heat and cover, stirring the mixture from time to time to prevent it from sticking.

4. Check the mixture after 15–20 minutes to make sure all the apple has broken down. If not, return to the heat and check again every 2 minutes.

APPLE SWIRLS

Ingredients

- scant 1 cup (200 ml / 7 fl oz) apple sauce (see above)
- 3 chopped Medjool dates or a handful of raisins
- 1/2 teaspoon cinnamon
- 1 sheet of store-bought puff pastry

1. Preheat the oven to 400°F (200°C).

2. Mix together the apple sauce, the dates or raisins, and cinnamon.

3. Spoon the apple sauce mix into the center of the rolled-out pastry. Keep a 1/3 in (1 cm) lip around the edge of the pastry free from any sauce.

4. Roll the pastry up from the long side, as if it was a roll of wallpaper.

5. Remove any sauce which may have dripped out of the sides (and while no one is looking, eat it).

6. Cut into 1 in (2 1/2 cm) pieces and lay on a baking sheet, leaving room between each one to allow for spreading.

7. Cook for 10–15 minutes, or until the swirls have turned golden brown.

Main image Rose hips.
Inset Wild roses can have white to dark pink flowers.

ROSE *ROSA* SPECIES

A thorny shrub, measuring 3–10 ft (1–3 m) high (or higher when they grow into trees) with very distinctive large flowers, bright red fruits known as hips, and sharp, hooked thorns.

Leaves
Dark green leaves with a serrated edge. They have a single leaflet on the end and one to three further pairs of leaflets, all ²/₃–1¹/₂ in (1¹/₂–4 cm) long and ¹/₃ to ³/₄ in (1–2 cm) wide.

Flowers
Cultivated roses come in all colors, shapes, and sizes. The wild rose has a white to dark pink flower, with the bottom or inner part of the petals often remaining white. They have a large yellow stamen, and flower in the late spring and into the summer.

Fruit
Bright red fruit known as hips, the shape of a small, misshapen football. Or for the rugged rose (*Rosa rugosa*), they look like a slightly flattened tomato with elongated calyx (see wild blueberry, page 64). They fruit in the fall.

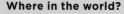

Where in the world?
Throughout North America and Europe.

Where to find it locally
In hedgerows, gardens, parks, and edgeland. *Rosa rugosa* can also be found in coastal regions.

HOW TO EAT IT

Pick the petals rather than the whole flower so it will fruit. Petals can be used in salads, in desserts, or to make rose water, which can in turn be used to make Turkish delight sweets and rose lemonade. Use the whole hip for tea (let it steep for 10 minutes or more), or make rose hip jelly, syrup, or cordial. Can also be used in savory dishes. In all cases, avoid the irritating hairs that grow on the seeds.

TO DRY ROSE PETALS

1. Bake in the oven on a non-stick tray for 10 minutes at 195°F (90°C).

2. Alternatively, dry them in a microwave between sheets of paper towel for 40 seconds on a high setting.

ROSE PETAL SCOOKIES*

Ingredients
- ½ cup (125 ml / 4 fl oz) coconut milk
- ½ cup (125 ml / 4 fl oz) natural yogurt (you can use vegan yogurt)
- ⅓ cup (65 g / 2¼ oz) semolina
- ¼ teaspoon rose water
- 2 tablespoons dried rose petals
- ¼ cup (25 g / 1 oz) chopped pistachio nuts
- 1 tablespoon honey
- ½ teaspoon baking powder
- 1 cup (155 g / 5 oz) self-rising flour
- maple syrup or rose syrup, to drizzle

*Scookies are a cross between a scone and a cookie.

1. Preheat the oven to 350°F (175°C).

2. Combine the coconut milk, yogurt, semolina, and rose water together in a large bowl.

3. Add the rose petals, chopped nuts, and honey.

4. Stir in the baking powder and slowly stir through the flour.

5. Use a tablespoon to create balls about 2 in (5 cm) large and place on a greased baking tray.

6. Bake for 20 minutes or until golden brown.

7. Remove from the oven, prick each cookie with a fork, and drizzle liberally with the maple or rose syrup.

8. Serve warm with ice cream, or as a scone with butter and rose jam.

HAWTHORN *CRATAEGUS MONOGYNA*

A large shrub or small tree growing 16½–49 ft (5–15 m) tall. It has brilliant white blossom in the early spring followed by a small apple-like berry. There are always thorns on the branches.

Other names
European hawthorn, common hawthorn.

Leaves
Leaves vary according to species. With common or European hawthorn (*Crataegus monogyna*), the leaves are around 2½ in (6 cm) with toothed edges and lobes which can go right into the central rib, giving them the appearance of a tiny Christmas tree. Other species lack these lobes and their leaves look more like an apple tree leaf: oval shaped with toothed edges.

Blossom
It has white blossom with five petals in the spring.

Fruit
A haw or hawthorn berry looks like a small red apple, growing on a stalk with a star-shaped calyx on the bottom (see wild blueberry, page 64). They are ripe in the late summer and throughout the fall. The European hawthorn is around the size of a pea and has a single seed.

What to avoid
It should not be mistaken for bryony, which is a vine that can wind itself through hedges (including hawthorn hedges). Bryony berries grow on the vine, so always double check that the hawthorn berries are on the hawthorn tree; look for thorns, an apple-like fruit, and a seed in the fruit. Avoid red berries which grow in umbrella-shaped clusters (in the same way elderberry does).

Where in the world?
Crataegus monogyna can be found throughout Europe, and has been introduced into parts of North America. There are a bewildering number of different wild hawthorns, all of which are edible (as long as you remove the seed), but they vary in flavor.

Where to find it locally
It is a common hedgerow plant. Also found in parks, gardens, and in edgeland.

HOW TO EAT IT

The leaves can be eaten in the spring as they are just emerging, but grow bitter after this time. The berries are very versatile and can be eaten raw or cooked; the seed needs to be removed or spat out when eating (do this outside!) as they are somewhat poisonous. Haws or hawthorn berries can be cooked in a little apple juice (just enough to cover them), and then pushed through a sieve. This mixture can then be made into a jam or into a ketchup, or it can be dehydrated (use an oven on a low temperature or a dehydrator) to make fruit leather.

HAWTHORN ENERGY BALLS

Ingredients

- 4 cups (400 g / 14 oz) hawthorn berries (haws)
- 4 tablespoons oats
- generous pinch of cinnamon
- 1 tablespoon maple syrup or honey
- a pinch of grated lemon zest
- ground almonds or ground nuts/seeds of your choice

1. Put a strong sieve over a bowl and push the hawthorn berries through it. It can seem like nothing is happening for a while as it all collects on the bottom of the sieve like a layer of ketchup. You'll need to use a butter knife or bendy spatula to scrape it off and put it in the bowl. If you find it hard to push them all through, ask your grown-up to do this part.

2. You should be left with lots of stalks, skins and seeds in the sieve and a thick, ketchup-like goo in the bottom of the bowl. From 4 cups (400 g / 14 oz) of hawthorn berries you will get around 1 cup (100 g / 3½ oz) of hawthorn goo.

3. Stir in the rest of the ingredients, except the ground nuts or seeds. It should be the consistency of putty or play dough; if not, add a pinch of ground almonds/seeds.

4. Roll into balls about the size of a small walnut.

5. Roll in ground almonds/seeds to coat.

6. Arrange on a plate and place in the refrigerator for around an hour to harden up.

BLACK RASPBERRY *RUBUS OCCIDENTALIS* (USA);
RASPBERRY, *RUBUS IDAEUS* (EUROPE)

A shrub with a long, hard stem known as a cane, and black or pinkish red fruit. It grows up to 6½ ft (2 m) high, and is commonly found on the edges of woodland and in woodland clearings.

Leaves
The leaves are light green on top and silvery green underneath with toothed edges. Each leaf is made of three to five smaller leaflets, with the largest at the end in the middle, at right angles to the other two, which are opposite each other. The leaves have small thorns on them.

Flowers
It flowers around the middle of summer. The flowers are white or pink and have five petals and five sepals, which grow under the petals in a star shape. In some species, such as the *Rubus occidentalis* or black raspberry, the green sepals are twice as long as the white petals, and as the name might suggest, the fruit is black when ripe.

Fruit
The fruit is a cluster of small red balls known as drupelets, which grow around a central core to form a black or pinkish red berry. It differs from other fruit in this plant family, such as blackberries, as it is hollow in the middle. They can range from ⅓–¾ in (1–2 cm) in length. The fruit comes toward the end of summer or in the early fall.

Where in the world?
Across Europe and North America, but absent from the southern states, from Texas east to Florida.

Opposite The fruits of the wild raspberry, *Rubus idaeus*, are often smaller than the cultivated raspberry, but just as tasty.

Left The black raspberry, *Rubus occidentalis*, grows in the United States. It has similar leaves to the raspberry but with black fruit and a pricklier stem.

Where to find it locally

Raspberries grow in hedgerows and toward the edges of woodland. They also escape from gardens and areas where people grow fruits, such as small farms and community gardens.

HOW TO EAT IT

Raspberries are best eaten straight from the cane. They can also be made into jams, added to ice cream or to your favorite breakfast cereal, made into smoothies (mix with banana, yogurt, and your favorite milk), or placed on the top of cakes as a decoration.

GLUTEN-FREE RASPBERRY MUFFINS

Ingredients
- 1 ⅓ cups (125 g / 4½ oz) chickpea flour
- ⅓ cup (70 g / 2½ oz) superfine sugar (preferably golden)
- 1 teaspoon baking powder
- ½ teaspoon baking soda
- ½ teaspoon cinnamon
- pinch of salt
- 1 egg (or 4 tablespoons vegan yogurt)
- 1 teaspoon vanilla extract
- scant ½ cup (100 ml / 3½ fl oz) apple sauce
- 3 tablespoons vegetable oil (rapeseed/canola)
- grated zest of 1 lemon
- 2 teaspoons lemon juice
- ½ cup (25 g) raspberries

1. Preheat the oven to 375°F (190°C).

2. Sift the chickpea flour into a large mixing bowl.

3. Add the sugar, baking powder, baking soda, cinnamon, and salt, and mix together.

4. If using an egg, beat it in a separate bowl.

5. Add the vanilla extract, apple sauce and vegetable oil to the bowl with the egg (or add the vegan yogurt, if using).

6. Combine the bowl of wet ingredients with the dry ingredients.

7. Stir through the lemon zest and juice, then fold in the raspberries.

8. Pour into eight baking cups lined with cupcake liners and bake for 20 minutes; if you are using the vegan yogurt instead of the egg, bake for 25 minutes.

9. Allow to cool, then serve. They go well with ice cream (what doesn't?).

BEECH *FAGUS SYLVATICA*

Beech trees can grow to around 115 ft (35 m) tall, but you will often find them a lot smaller, around 29½ ft (9 m) or about the height of a house. When in leaf they are dome shaped. Once the leaves die back in the fall, they often stay on the tree until a strong wind blows them off.

Leaves
The leaves are wavy and lime green, or even slightly silver, and a little hairy when they emerge. They grow to 1½–3½ in (4–9 cm) and lose their hairs as they mature. They are oval-shaped and wavy with a pointy tip.

Flowers
Beech is what's known as "monoecious," which is a long word meaning male and female flowers grow on the tree at the same time as catkins and blossom. The catkins are long, droopy clusters of flowers which dangle off the tree like hundreds of earrings. The flowers are light brown (or red on a copper beech tree) and green and grow in pairs. They don't stay as flowers for long, turning into little green furry balls which develop into the casing of the nut.

Fruit or nut
A hard, four-sided furry case which will open when the nut is ripe. The nut has three sides and looks like a mini-chestnut; you get one or two of them in a case. If the flower has not been pollinated, the nuts are flat and contain no fleshy bit to eat.

Where in the world?
Fagus sylvatica grows in the northeastern part of the United States. It also grows in southeast England, southeast Wales, and throughout Europe with the exception of northern Scandinavia, Portugal, and all but the northern coast of Spain. *Fagus grandifolia* grows all over the eastern United States, as far west as Texas and Minnesota or Ontario in Canada.

Where to find it locally
In beech woods, parks, gardens, and sometimes planted along streets.

How to eat it
You can eat the first leaves of a beech when they are still very small and silvery or light green. Don't be tempted to eat the older, darker green leaves, as these will contain lots of tannins, which can make you sick; thankfully it is hard to eat too much of them as they taste disgusting! Beech nuts, often called beech mast, make a very tasty snack. They can also be toasted in a warm oven (see hazelnut, page 118, but cook for half the time). Beech nuts should be peeled as the skins can be bitter and astringent, and not good for you in large quantities.

CEP *BOLETUS EDULIS*

Ceps are also called penny buns as the top of the mushroom can look like a bread roll. The stem is bulbous and they grow from 2 in (5 cm) in height to 14 in (35 cm), though most are around 5 in (13 cm) tall.

Other names
Porcini, penny bun, king bolete.

Pores not gills
Ceps are known as a polypore mushroom, meaning they have no gills but instead hundreds of tiny pores or tubes on the underside of the cap, a little like a sponge. The pores do not change color when the mushroom is cut or bruised. They should be off-white or creamy, turning yellow as the cep grows older and goes off. The pores should not contain any pink.

Cap
The cap is dark brown, resembling a cooked bread bun, hence the name. They often have white patches where insects have had a little munch on them. The cap has a fine velvety appearance.

Stem
There is a fine white mesh pattern (lattice) on the top of the stem nearest the cap. The stem is also usually more bulbous at the bottom. It is generally very robust and fat in relation to the overall size of the mushroom (as opposed to slender and tall).

What to avoid
Avoid any mushroom without the white mesh pattern on the top of the stem. Avoid any mushroom which stains when cut (especially if the stain is blue or reddish). Also avoid mushrooms with red or pinkish pores, ones with gills, or those growing under hemlock spruces or near busy roads. Always smell the mushroom. Ceps can remain in the ground for a couple of weeks, slowly decomposing. The mushroom should smell nice and mushroomy! If it doesn't, it's either gone bad or is a different species. As with all mushrooms, only eat them if you are 100% sure.

Where in the world?
In woodlands across North America and Europe.

Where to find it locally
If you find these mushrooms it is best to keep their whereabouts secret, as they grow in the same place each year and are highly sought after. They can be found at the edges of woods, especially birch, beech, oak, and pine. They normally come up toward the end of the summer.

HOW TO EAT IT

This delicious mushroom is great fried in a little butter, made into a soup, or added to a risotto. Ceps go well with cheese, and as they are high in protein they are particularly suitable for vegetarian and vegan dishes. Drying ceps both enhances the flavor and preserves the mushroom. Simply cut them into pieces, thread them onto a string, and hang up above a radiator. Store in airtight jars afterward.

CEP AND VEGETABLE SOUP

Ingredients

- 1⅓ cups (100 g / 3½ oz) chopped fresh ceps or ⅜ cup (30 g / 1 oz) dried ceps
- 1 tablespoon vegetable oil
- 1 onion, chopped
- 1 garlic clove, crushed
- 3 cups (750 ml / 1¼ pints) water
- 2 teaspoons bouillon powder or vegetable stock or 1 mushroom stock cube
- 1 carrot, cut into ribbons using a vegetable peeler*
- 1½ teaspoons shoyu sauce, mild soy sauce, or liquid aminos
- 2 nests (120 g / 4 oz) of egg or rice noodles
- chives to decorate (optional)

*No matter how hard you try, it is impossible to cut the whole carrot into ribbons; you will more than likely be left with a carrot core to munch on!

1. If using dried mushrooms, place them in a bowl or pan, cover in boiling water and let them steep for 30 minutes.

2. Heat the oil and fry the onions until they start to brown, then add the garlic to the browned onions.

3. Pour the water over the onions and stir in the stock.

4. Add the mushrooms to the mix along with the carrot ribbons.

5. Add the shoyu, soy sauce, or liquid aminos and simmer for 10 minutes or so, or until the carrot softens.

6. Add the noodles and cook until they are soft (3–5 minutes, depending on the type of noodle; follow the packet instructions).

7. Pour into bowls and sprinkle on some chopped chives, if using.

SQUIRRELS
It can be difficult to beat the squirrels to these delicious nuts. However, I have found that squirrels do not always like crossing roads, and in urban areas those growing on traffic islands can be the most abundant.

HAZELNUT *CORYLUS AVELLANA*

Small green, ripening to brown, nuts with a green fading to brown casing growing on a deciduous tree, reaching up to 40 ft (12 m), although usually smaller as it is coppiced.

Leaves
Leaves grow to about the size of a palm (not including fingers) of an adult hand. They are oval or round, slightly hairy, and have a point at the tip. They also have doubly serrated edges which resemble a saw or bread knife.

Flowers
The flowers are tiny, red, almost insignificant structures, which are seldom seen. The large droopy yellowish catkins are a far better way to identify the plant.

Nuts
The outer shell of a hazelnut is around 1/3–1 in (1½–2½ cm) long and a little over half as wide. It is dark brown and tapers to a point. The shell has a light brown, almost gray ring where it joins the sheath. The inside nut has a papery casing and a light interior. Hazelnuts are attached to the tree by a light green sheath (an involucre), which turns brown as the nut ripens. The involucre differs for different species; it can cover the nut completely, fan out, or be almost non-existent.

Where in the world?
In the United States you will find the European hazel (*Corylus avellana*) along with the American hazelnut (*Corylus americana*) and the beaked hazelnut (*Corylus cornuta*), both of which have long sheaths or involucres over the nut. Hazel trees grow all over Europe.

Where to find it locally
Found in and at the edges of woodlands, in hedgerows, and on some edgeland.

HOW TO EAT IT

Keep one step ahead of the squirrels and pick the nuts when green or just starting to brown; then allow them to ripen in a warm, dry, dark place. Use nutcrackers or two stones to crack the nuts. Eat as a snack or add to muesli or flapjacks. They can be made into hazelnut milk by soaking the nuts overnight; discard the water, blend the nuts and fresh water (using a ratio of 3:1 water to nuts) in a blender, strain and serve. You can sweeten this with dates or maple syrup, or add cocoa powder to make chocolate hazelnut milk.

HAZELNUT CHOCOLATE SPREAD

Ingredients

- ²/₃ cup (100 g / 3½ oz) shelled hazelnuts
- 2 teaspoons cocoa powder
- 3 tablespoons vegetable oil (rapeseed/canola)
- 3 teaspoons maple syrup

1. Preheat the oven to 400°F (200°C).

2. Put the shelled hazelnuts onto a baking tray, then place in the top of the oven for 8–12 minutes, or until the skins start to darken.

3. Remove the hazelnuts from the oven and let them cool on a plate.

4. Once they have cooled down, rub off the skins.

5. Place in a clean coffee grinder, seed grinder, or a pestle and mortar and grind to a powder. You may end up with one or two lumps, but if most of it is powder, it will be fine.

6. Pour into a large bowl and thoroughly mix in the remaining ingredients. Serve on toast or crackers.

SWEET CHESTNUT *CASTANEA SATIVA*

A very large woodland tree, reaching heights of 115 ft (35 m), they can live for up to 700 years! They have long serrated leaves and the dark brown pointed nuts are in light green spiky cases.

Leaves
The leaves are long, measuring 4–10 in (10–25 cm) and have fifteen pairs of parallel veins. They also have very prominent serrated edges, like the teeth of a saw.

Flowers
Chestnuts have catkins, long yellow clusters of flowers which can look like fireworks bursting out of the tree.

Fruit
Chestnuts look a little like a conker (horse chestnut), but as conkers are poisonous it is worth knowing the difference.
Here is a checklist to help; if you consider every point on the list rather than just one or two, that way you will be certain you have a chestnut and not a conker.

CHESTNUTS 2–3 in a case (usually 3)	CONKER/HORSE CHESTNUT 1–2 in a case (usually 1)
Always has a flat side	Normally completely round; will only have a flat side if there are 2 in the case
Has a point at the bottom	No point at the bottom
Tend to stay in case when they fall	Tend to fall out of the case
Lots of long little prickles on the case	Few stubby prickles on the case
Leaves are single	Leaves form a hand shape

Where in the world?
Found in eastern North America and across Europe, with the exception of Norway and Finland.

Where to find it locally
In mature woodland, parks and gardens.

HOW TO EAT IT

The easiest way to eat a chestnut is to roast it. On the flat side, score a cross with a sharp knife on all but one of the chestnuts. Put them into a hot oven (400°F/200°C) until you hear a pop. This will be the unscored chestnut popping, and that is the sign the others are ready. You may not hear the popping, so check after 15 minutes, then again every 5 minutes. If they are cooked, they should be slightly brown inside and soft when stabbed with a knife.

SWEET POTATO AND CHESTNUT BURGERS

Ingredients
- 1 small (400 g / 14 oz) peeled sweet potato
- 1⅓ cups (180 g / 6 oz) roasted, shelled chestnuts
- generous ¾ cup (100 g / 3½ oz) of ground roasted beech nuts (remove skins if you can) or ground almonds
- 3 teaspoons tomato purée
- 1 teaspoon soy sauce or liquid aminos
- 1 teaspoon Italian herbs
- 1 teaspoon smoked paprika (optional)
- some flour for forming the burgers

1. Preheat the oven to 350°F (180°C).

2. Chop the sweet potato, then place it in a pan of boiling water for 10–12 minutes until it is soft.

3. In a large bowl, mash the sweet potato and chestnuts together using a potato masher.

4. Sprinkle in the ground nuts and add the tomato purée, soy sauce, and flavorings.

5. On a floured service, work the mix into individual burgers.

6. Bake for 25–30 minutes, until browned and slightly hardened.

SMOOTH SUMAC

Smooth sumac has berries which are
pinky red in color with a dusting of gray
from their tiny hairs. The berries are not
round but slightly flat, more like a lentil.
Unlike the staghorn sumac, the stems
are smooth. These berries can be used
in the same way as berries from
a staghorn sumac.

STAGHORN SUMAC *RHUS TYPHINA*

A small tree or shrub with furry branches and brilliant purple clusters of furry berries known as drupes. The drupes stay on the plant over winter.

Leaves
Leaf-sized leaflets grow opposite each other (in seven to twelve pairs) on a central leaf stalk with a single leaflet pointing out at the end. These radiate from a single point with the characteristic purple drupe spike in the middle. In the fall the leaves turn from green, through yellow and orange, to a bright vivid red before darkening and dropping.

Fruit
The flame-shaped drupe points upwards, comprising hundreds of tiny furry dark maroon berries. They measure 5–8 in (12–20 cm) long and 1½–2 in (4–6 cm) wide at the base. Fruit will stay on the tree until spring.

Other identifying features
The branches are furry and resemble the antlers of a reindeer or stag, which is how the plant gets its name.

What to avoid
Poison sumac (*Toxicodendron vernix*) has loosely packed white drupes rather than bright maroon. The tree of heaven (*Ailanthus altissima*) has similar leaves, but clusters of drooping seeds rather than upright maroon drupes.

Where in the world?
Staghorn sumac grows wild in the northwestern United States and southeast Canada; it also grows in gardens and parks throughout Europe. Smooth sumac (*Rhus glabra*) grows all over the United States.

Where to find it locally
Find it in parks and gardens, also backing on to edgeland and wasteland where it has "escaped" from gardens.

HOW TO EAT IT

Sumac drupes have a wonderful lemon flavor. They can be rubbed carefully against a sieve to produce sumac powder, which can be used on hummus and in other Middle Eastern cooking.

SUMAC LEMONADE

Sumac lemonade is an easy and rewarding recipe; it needs little in the way of preparation and there are very few ingredients to make this delicious pink lemonade-like drink.

Ingredients

- sumac drupes, picked in the late summer or fall
- maple syrup, honey, or sugar (optional)

1. Place the sumac drupes in a pan and cover with water. Give them a good squeeze.

2. Bring to a boil, then remove from the heat.

3. Leave to infuse for around 1 hour; the mixture should be really pink. If it is at all gray, the drupes have been on the plant for too long and the flavor will be too poor to drink.

4. Pour the mixture through a sieve lined with a muslin cloth or coffee filter.

5. Serve in a tall glass over ice, adding maple syrup, honey, or sugar if it is too tart.

WINTER

Evergreen leaves like wood sorrel and sea beet can be good to eat in the cold winter months. At the very end of winter, make the most of the sweet rising sap of the birch tree.

WOOD SORREL *OXALIS STRICTA* (USA); *OXALIS ACETOSELLA* (EUROPE)

Wood sorrel looks a little like clover. It is a very common woodland plant, growing low on the woodland floor. The North American yellow-flowered wood sorrel (*Oxalis stricta*) grows to around 6 in (15 cm). The European wood sorrel (*Oxalis acetosella*) is quite small, measuring only 2–4 in (5–10 cm) high.

Leaves

Three heart shapes on a single stalk. The leaves can be a little hairy, and will fold flat at night and open in the morning. Clover can look similar, but this has oval-shaped leaves.

Flowers

The flowers of *Oxalis acetosella* are white with pinky-purple veins; they have five petals and are quite small, measuring around $\frac{1}{3}$–$\frac{2}{3}$ in (1–1$\frac{1}{2}$ cm). In North America *Oxalis stricta* is more common; it has yellow flowers. In France and the UK you may also find the yellow-flowered New Zealand wood sorrel, *Oxalis exilis*.

Fruit

White-flowered wood sorrel (*Oxalis acetosella*) has tiny rounded fruits (a little over $\frac{1}{8}$ in / 4 mm) with five flat edges. The North American yellow-flowered wood sorrel (*Oxalis stricta*) has longer fruits, almost like a square-sided pea-pod with a point at the end, and the New Zealand wood sorrel (*Oxalis exilis*) has fruits the shape of a rugby ball.

Where in the world?

Oxalis stricta is found in the eastern and northwestern parts of the United States and in eastern Canada. *Oxalis acetosella* is found across Europe and in the eastern United States. *Oxalis exilis* can be found in the UK and France.

Opposite Wood sorrel, *Oxalis acetosella* (Europe).

Left North American yellow-flowered wood sorrel, *Oxalis stricta*, is found in parts of the United States and Canada.

Where to find it locally

As you might guess, with a name like "wood" sorrel it is most commonly found in woodland, but also in shady hedgerows and gardens.

How to eat it

These three wood sorrels have a sharp lemony flavor and taste a little like grape or apple skins. They are best picked and eaten straight away as a snack. You can also throw a few leaves into a salad or wilt it down over green beans.

SEA BEET *BETA VULGARIS SSP. MARITIMA*

Sea beet is the wild ancestor of beets; it grows in clumps on the coast and is one of the few edible green leaves which can be found all year round. The clumps are in a rosette form, the leaves surrounding a central point. They are around 1–1½ ft (30–45 cm) high before they are in flower, with a flowering spike which measures over 3 ft (1 m) high.

Leaves

The leaves are glossy, smooth to the touch, and triangular, resembling a spade symbol on a deck of cards, but with straight rather than rounded sides at the end nearest the stalk. They are light to darkish green in color, occasionally having reddish-purple markings, rather like a beet leaf.

Flowers

The plant sends up a flowering spike in the spring with many green flowers with no petals clustered together. These flowers can sometimes have hints of the reddish-purple shades of the beet.

Fruit

The fruits are small clusters which fade in color, holding a small black seed.

Where in the world?

Found on the coast of California, in the northeast from Virginia to Massachusetts, and throughout coastal Europe.

Where to find it locally

It grows next to the sea on the edge of beaches. Like all foraged leaves it should be washed well, especially if people walk dogs in the area. Be careful when picking on high cliffs.

WINTER

HOW TO EAT IT

Small, young leaves are the best; never take more than you need, especially in the winter. Treat sea beet as you would spinach; it goes very well with cream cheese (most things do!), in a quiche or flan, with pasta, or in soups. The simplest way to use it is to wilt it in a pan with a little butter and perhaps a drop or two of balsamic vinegar. It works very well in Indian cooking.

SEA BEET HUFF-A-PUFFS

Ingredients
- ²/₃ cup (150 g / 5 oz) sea beet leaves (stalks removed)
- ¹/₃ cup (75 g / 2³/₄ oz) cream cheese
- a good pinch of nutmeg
- 1 sheet of store-bought puff pastry
- a little milk, for brushing

1. Preheat the oven to 375°F (190°C).

2. Wilt the sea beet in a pan over low heat, then allow to cool, squeeze out the juice, and chop.

3. In a bowl, mix the sea beet with the cream cheese and nutmeg.

4. Cut the sheet of pastry into twelve equal-sized roughly square pieces.

5. Using a tablespoon, put half of the mix into the center of each of the squares.

6. Fold in the corners of each square so they meet in the middle, then brush each with a little milk.

7. Place in the top of the oven for 15–20 minutes, or until the pastry is golden brown.

SEA BEET'S RELATIONS

Sea beet is not only the ancestor of our common beet; it is also closely related to Swiss chard, sugar beet (used to make sugar), and an animal food crop known as mangel-wurzel.

BIRCH *BETULA PENDULA*

Birch trees grow to around 100 ft (30 m) tall. Most species have white bark with dashes on them (see "Trunk" below). They are among the first trees to colonize an area, so you often see them on wasteground or abandoned sites.

Leaves
The leaves are small and light green. They are shaped like a flattened flame: triangular with a point at the end, and spiky or toothed edges.

Catkins
Birch trees have both male and female catkins. The female catkins are small, green, and stick upright, while the male are long, yellow, and droop down.

Trunk
Young birch trees have distinctive horizontal lines on the trunk, as if someone has drawn a series of dashes. These are called lenticels and during the night they let in carbon dioxide and let out oxygen and water vapour. The bark can peel like sheets of paper. On older trees the bark can become darker and more bumpy, especially at the base.

Where in the world?
Silver birch (*Betula pendula*) is found in northeastern and northwestern United States and Canada, and throughout Europe.

Where to find it locally
Look for them in abandoned places, and also in young woodland, parks, and gardens.

HOW TO EAT IT

The young leaves of a birch are edible. The sap of the tree makes an excellent drink, or it can be reduced down to make birch syrup (see opposite).

TAPPING A BIRCH

During the late winter, when the snow melts and it gets above freezing in the day, birches are ready to tap. Make sure you have permission from the landowner first.

You will need:

- a sharp knife or cordless drill with wide bit (kids, you will need a grown-up to help)
- 3 in (7–8 cm) piece of plastic tubing (or specialist birch tap)
- a large jug or bucket
- a cork (or similar) to plug up the hole
- moss or candle wax, to plug any gaps

1. Find a tree with a trunk over 1 ft (30 cm) in diameter.

2. Drill a hole into the trunk about 2 ft (60 cm) up; only go just under the bark layer.

3. Insert the tubing or birch tap into the hole, and run the other end into a jug or bucket—support the container with stones or dug-in twigs if necessary. Leave overnight.

4. The container should be full or filling up by the morning; replace it with a new container if you wish to collect more.

5. Seal off the hole with a cork, rubber stopper or a piece of twig the size of the hole, and plug up any gaps with moss or ideally candle wax.

6. Birch sap should be clear; if it's brown or yellow it may be infected and you should discard the liquid.

MAKING BIRCH SYRUP

For every 4 cups (1 liter / 1³⁄₄ pints) of sap, you may end up with just 2 teaspoons (10 ml) of syrup, so just 1 percent of the original volume. This process can take up to 3 days, depending on how much sap you have. Start with small amounts, such as 4 cups (1 liter / 1³⁄₄ pints), as this will only take 6–8 hours, and work up to larger amounts.

Some birches are sweeter than others: use the sweet ones for pancakes and the more bitter ones as you would balsamic vinegar. We advise keeping the syrup away from dogs.

1. In a large pan, bring the sap to a boil and boil half the liquid away.

2. Reduce the heat or transfer the sap to a slow cooker and set to low. Check regularly, ensuring it never boils.

3. After each 2 hours, pass through a coffee filter and continue to heat. When it's at 10 percent of the original volume, it can be cooled and used as a sweet drink. Otherwise, continue with the instructions below for a syrup.

4. Repeat until the liquid thickens; it will be like a runny batter in consistency, rather than thick like maple syrup. Pour into a jar and cool.

Above When at 10 percent volume, the sap can be cooled as a drink.

INDEX

Page numbers in *italics* refer
to directory main entries.

A

allergic reactions, 12
apple, *94–97*
  apple sauce, 96
  apple swirls, 96
apps, 13

B

bags, 13
baking trays, 22
beech, *110–111*
beet, 135
  sea, *132–135*
  sugar, 135
berry pickers, 13
bilberry, *64–67*
  wild blueberry flapjack, 67, 82
  see also blueberry, wild
birch, *136–139*
  making birch syrup, 139
  tapping a birch, 138
blackberry, *88–91*
  blackberry cheesecake, 90
blueberry, wild, *64–67*
  wild blueberry flapjack, 67, 82
  see also bilberry
boots, 13

C

calyxes, 64
cep, *112–115*
  cep and vegetable
  soup, 115
chard, Swiss, 135
cherry
  bird, 56, 59
  ice pops, 59
  sour, 59
  wild, *56–59*
chestnut
  horse, 120
  sweet, *120–123*
  sweet potato and chestnut burgers, 123
chickweed, *42–43*
  chickweed dip, 42
clothing, 13
coasts, 15
coffee filters, 22
colanders, 22
conservation, 23
containers, 13
cooking food, 12
cupcake liners, 22

D

dandelions, *30–33*
  dandelion frittata, 32

E

edgeland, 20
elder, *60–63*
  elder shortbread, 63
  elderberry syrup, 62
equipment, 13
  kitchen equipment, 22

F

farmland, 21
fat hen, 39, 41
field guides, 12, 13
first-aid kits, 13
foraging, 9
  children, 9
  cost, 11
  freshness, 11
  safety considerations, 12
  what to wear, 13
  where to forage, 15–21
  why forage?, 10–11
forests, 16

G

gardens, 17
garlic mustard, *48–51*
  jumping jack wraps, 51
garlic, wild, *34–37*
  garlicky nettle pesto, 28
  wild ramps bread, 36
  wild ramps butter, 32, 36
  see also ramps, wild
glasswort, Virginia, *68–69*
  see also samphire, marsh
gloves, 13
goosefoot, *38–41*
  wilted goosefoot
  greens, 40
guide books, 12, 13

H

hawthorn, *102–105*
  hawthorn energy balls, 105
hazelnut, *116–119*
  hazelnut chocolate
  spread, 118
heaths, 18
hedgerows, 21

I

internet, 12

J

jack-by-the hedge, 48
  jumping jack wraps, 51

K

kitchen equipment, 22

L

local guides, 12

M

mangel-wurzel, 135
marsh samphire, *68–69*
  see also glasswort, Virginia
meadows, 21
measuring jugs, 22
measuring spoons and
    cups, 22
mint, *44–47*
  mint ice cubes, 47
  nettle and mint
    smoothie, 46
moors, 18
muslin cloths, 22

N

nettles, *26–29*, 36
  garlicky nettle pesto, 28
  nettle and mint
    smoothie, 46

O

O'Neill, Finley, 77

P

pants, 13
parks, 17
penny buns, 112
picnics, 13
plains, 18
plantain, *52–53*
  buck's horn, 52
plum
  beach, 87
  cherry, 87
  plums in honey and
    thyme, 87
  wild, *84–87*
pollution, 12
porcini, 112
public spaces, 17
puffball, giant, *74–77*
  puffball kebabs, 76

R

radish, wild, *78–79*
raincoats, 13

ramps, wild, *34–37*
  garlicky nettle pesto, 28
  wild ramps bread, 36
  wild ramps butter, 32, 36
  see also garlic, wild
raspberry, *106–109*
  black raspberry, *106–109*
  gluten-free raspberry muffins, 108
ribwort, 52
rose, *98–101*
  drying rose petals, 100
  rose petal scookies, 100

S

safety considerations, 12
samphire, marsh, *68–69*
  see also glasswort, Virginia
saucepans, 22
scales, 22
scissors, 13
sea beet, *132–135*
  sea beet huff-a-puffs, 134
sieves, 22
snacks, 13
sorrel
  common, *70–73*
  sheep's, *70–73*
  wood, *130–131*
  yogurt and sorrel dipping sauce, 72
spearmint, *44–47*
  mint ice cubes, 47
  nettle and mint
    smoothie, 46
squirrels, 116
strawberries, modern, 83
strawberry
  mock, 81
  Virginian, *80–83*
  wild strawberry
    cranachan, 82
  woodland, *80–83*
sumac
  poison, 125
  smooth, 124
  staghorn, *124–127*
  sumac lemonade, 126
sun protection, 13
sweet potato and chestnut burgers, 123

T

tree of heaven, 125

W

washing food, 12
water bottles, 13
whortleberry, *64–67*
woodlands, 16

ABOUT THE AUTHOR

David Hamilton has an incurable but thankfully mild obsession with edible plants. He has a degree in food science and nutrition and a diploma in sustainable horticulture. An avid forager, horticulturist, and magazine journalist, David is also the author of numerous books, including the *Wild Ruins* series of travel books and the cult classic gardening book *Grow Your Food for Free*. He began teaching foraging courses in 2007 after years of experimenting with wild foods. He has worked with organizations including the National Trust, the Eden Project, and Bristol Botanic Gardens, and has appeared on numerous TV programs foraging with the likes of Ben Fogle and Mary Berry.

THANKS TO

A special thanks to Anna Mumford for getting this project off the ground and tirelessly helping throughout its creation. A big thank you to Jo Watson for opening her kitchen to me and acting as a recipe consultant and food stylist. Thank you to Vivienne Evans for her hard work proofreading the early drafts. Thanks to my partner Liz, my children, Jo's family, and Al and Lydia Halcrow and family for taste testing and taking part in the photo shoots, and Anna Francis and her family for further recipe sampling. Thanks to Jason Ingram for his photos, Sara Mulvanny for her lovely illustrations, and the team at Quarto/White Lion including Andrew Dunn, Laura Bulbeck, Sarah Pyke, and Jessica Axe for their hard work throughout. And finally, thank you for buying my book!

PICTURE CREDITS

All illustrations, except for maps © Sara Mulvanny.

All photographs © Jason Ingram, except for the following:
23tl Arterra Picture Library/Alamy Stock Photo; 24 Creative Travel Projects/Shutterstock.com; 30 & 32 background Stephanie C Perry/Shutterstock.com; 35 James Aloysius Mahan V/Shutterstock.com; 38 & 40 background simona pavan/Shutterstock.com; 43 Martin Fowler/Shutterstock.com; 54 krutar/Shutterstock.com; 61 Dezajny/Shutterstock.com; 64 Maryna Pleshkun/Shutterstock.com; 65 & 66 background A&P / Alamy Stock Photo; 68 Ria Van Bennett/Shutterstock.com; 69 Courtesy Peggy Romfh, Lady Bird Johnson Wildflower Center; 70 & 72 background Simone Andress/Shutterstock.com; 71 FJAH/Shutterstock.com; 74 main & 76 background Mateusz Ðciborski/Alamy Stock Photo; 74 inset © Mark Steinmetz; 80 main Eileen Kumpf/Shutterstock.com; 80 inset & 82 background I_V_Y/Shutterstock.com; 88 & 90 background Igor Normann/Shutterstock.com; 92 Agenturfotografin/Shutterstock.com; 94 & 96 gengirl/Shutterstock.com; 98 inset & 100 PhotoHouse/Shutterstock.com; 103 & 105 Roel Meijer/Shutterstock.com; 106 & 108 background Beautiful landscape/Shutterstock.com; 107 Vadym Zaitsev/Shutterstock.com; 111 guentermanaus/Shutterstock.com; 113 & 115 swa182/Shutterstock.com; 116 & 118 background Martin Fowler/Shutterstock.com; 118 main Bob Gibbons/Alamy Stock Photo; 121 & 123 Bildagentur Zoonar GmbH/Shutterstock.com; 124 & 126 background Zeljko Vranjkovic/Shutterstock.com; 128 Subbotina Anna/Shutterstock.com; 131 Manfred Ruckszio/Shutterstock.com; 136 & 138 Shartik1963/Shuterstock.com; 139b natalia bulatova/Shutterstock.com.